APARTMENT BUILDING VALUATION, FINANCE AND INVESTMENT ANALYSIS

Real Estate for Professional Practitioners
DAVID CLURMAN, Editor

APARTMENT BUILDING VALUATION, FINANCE AND INVESTMENT ANALYSIS

DANIEL J. O'CONNELL
Real Estate Appraiser and Analyst
Los Angeles, California

A RONALD PRESS PUBLICATION

JOHN WILEY & SONS

NEW YORK • CHICHESTER • BRISBANE • TORONTO • SINGAPORE

Library of Congress Cataloging in Publication Data:

O'Connell, Daniel J.
    Apartment building valuation, finance, and investment analysis.

    (Real estate for professional practitioners,
ISSN 0190-1087)
    "A Ronald Press publication."
    Bibliography: p.
    Includes index.
    1. Apartment houses. 2. Real estate investment.

I. Title. II. Series.
HD1394.025   332.63'243   82-2806
ISBN 0-471-86523-0   AACR2
Printed in the United States of America

10 9 8 7 6 5 4 3 2 1

SERIES PREFACE

Since the end of World War II, tremendous changes have taken place in the business and residential real estate fields throughout the world. This has been evidenced not only by architectural changes, exemplified by the modern shopping center, but also in the many innovative financing responses that have enabled development of new structures and complexes, such as multiuse buildings. It can be expected that real estate development will speed in new directions at an ever increasing pace to match the oncoming needs of our time. With this perspective, the Real Estate for Professional Practitioners series has been developed in response to professional needs.

As real estate professional activities have become divided into specialties, because of intensive demand for expertise at all stages, so has there developed an increasing need for extensive training and continual education for persons directly involved or dealing in business ventures requiring detailed knowledge of realty procedures.

Perhaps no field of business endeavor is more in need of a series of professional books than real estate. Working in the practical world of business and residential construction and space utilization, or at advanced levels of college training covering these areas, one is constantly aware that too little of existing creative thinking has been transcribed into viable books. Many of the books that have been written do not thoroughly enough encompass both the practical and theoretical aspects of complex subjects. Too often the drive for immediate answers has led to the overlooking of fundamental purposes and technical know-how that might lead to much more favorable results for the persons seeking knowledge.

This series will be made up of books thoroughly and expertly expounding existing procedures in the many fields of real estate, but searching as well for innovative solutions to current and future problems. These books are intended to offer a compendium of each author's wide experience and knowledge to aid the seasoned professional.

The series is addressed to professionals in all walks of realty endeavor. These include business investors and developers, urban affairs specialists, attorneys, accountants, and the many others whose work involves real estate creativity and investment. Just as importantly, the series will present to advanced students in many realty fields the opportunity to review professional thinking that will help to stimulate their own thoughts on modern trends in housing and business construction.

We believe these goals can be achieved by the outstanding group of authors who will create the books in the series.

DAVID CLURMAN

PREFACE

For the past few decades apartment buildings have been the most often built, appraised, loaned on, purchased, owned, and sold type of real estate other than owner-occupied dwellings and raw land. They probably have produced more millionaires than any other type of real estate investment. Huge numbers of buyers count themselves in the running for the relatively few buildings that do come on the market, often pushing prices so high that they create cash-flow whirlpools. Is this justifiable? What is the proper price to pay? Precisely what is the value of the tax shelter benefit? What is the bottom line effect of creative financing?

These are important questions that often go unanswered in the frenzied anticipation of riding the same great wave of property appreciation that produced so many instant geniuses in the 1970s. However, the game has now become more complicated. It is now a matter of structuring the deal properly, estimating value in the confusion of creative and unique financing, making educated decisions, and outwitting the competition. The trend clearly has been one of increasing education—the real pros are immersing themselves in knowledge through reading books and periodicals as well as through hard work in the classroom. The purpose of this book is to provide an introduction to apartment building investments and to present the analytical tools required for decision making.

The book is divided into four sections. Part 1 (Valuation) deals with basic valuation techniques, their considerations and pitfalls, the construction of income and expense statements, and property inspection. An understanding of these topics is essential to the seller in determining selling price. Part 2 (Investment Analysis) presents the discounted cash flow method for analyzing the apartment building investment and is of interest to the potential purchaser who wishes not only to see how profitable an investment might be, but who also has to make decisions between different investment opportunities and management strategies. The techniques in Part 2 are becoming more and more popular with the proliferation of small computers.

Part 3 (Financing) begins with an overview of various debt instruments, terminology, and techniques. Chapter 15 measures the actual return on a loan to the lender and is of great value in structuring the financing and persuading a lender or seller to make the loan. Chapter 16 covers cash equivalence—a valuable technique for determining the current cash value of creative or favorable financing. Computing loan point charges is also discussed. Chapters 17 and 18 discuss tax-deferred exchanges and installment sales.

Part 4 is dedicated entirely to report writing and includes outlines and samples of valuation and analysis reports. An additional purpose of the sample reports is to familiarize the reader with the valuation and analysis processes. In fact, reading these reports prior to studying Parts 1 and 2 is strongly suggested.

Seven calculator procedures are outlined in the Appendix. These procedures can be accomplished with one of several widely available, inexpensive, hand-held financial calculators that facilitate the computation of loan payments, loan balances, present values, future values, rates of return, and the effective interest rate on a loan.

By presenting these topics, this book acquaints the reader with the anatomy of a real estate investment from purchase through holding period and on to final disposition of the property. Equity growth is followed closely. You will learn how to determine the amount of tax shelter afforded by the investment, how to incorporate its value using a specific investor's tax bracket, and how to compute both before- and after-tax cash flows and the rate of return.

Although this book is geared specifically to apartment building investments, the principles are equally applicable to other real estate investments. In fact, the analysis techniques are especially relevant to office buildings, warehouses, and shopping centers where contracted rents, indexed income increases, and lease expirations cause varying income patterns unique to each property. The only differences are in the income and expense projections and in minor modifications of allowable depreciation methods.

A substantial portion of the book deals with federal tax law. Care should be taken to update this information as required. In performing after-tax cash flow projections as demonstrated in this book, it has been customary to omit state income tax consequences. However, they can be included in the analysis, and will add a further degree of refinement to the process.

These methods have long been recognized and used by professional appraisers, analysts, and consultants. May they bring you the highest return in money and professional gratification.

DANIEL J. O'CONNELL

Los Angeles, California
June 1982

ACKNOWLEDGMENTS

Thanks to my various mentors and associates, past and present, for their teaching patience, sharing of philosophies, thought-provoking questions, and challenges to my own work and ideas.

Thanks to Robert L. Foreman, SREA, MAI, and James J. Mason, MAI, whose classroom teaching and extraordinary enthusiasm helped kindle my own interest for the subjects contained in this book.

Thanks to the many real estate professionals who have shared their knowledge through many enlightening articles and books.

Thanks to G. Lindsay Hassiepen, whose suggestions and editing improved the manuscript and my writing skills.

Thanks to my family and friends, who have given me their continuing support—many times unknowingly. Special thanks to my parents for encouraging my reading and writing at an early age, even when the subject matter didn't meet with their approval.

D.J.O'C.

CONTENTS

PART THREE   FINANCING

PART 4   REPORT WRITING

APARTMENT BUILDING VALUATION, FINANCE AND INVESTMENT ANALYSIS

PART ONE

VALUATION

CHAPTER ONE

INCOME AND EXPENSES

Apartment buildings are not bought for the land and improvements, but *for the income* they generate. The focal point for either the valuation or investment analysis process is the *income and expense statement,* also called the *operating statement* or *pro forma.*

The income and expense statement is just what its name implies: it lists the income, expenses, and resulting net income experienced by a property over a one-year period. An income and expense statement for the previous year's building operation is a must when valuating or analyzing; better yet, statements should be obtained for the past three years. The income and expense statement for Case Study 1 (Chapter 13) provides a good format to use in the construction of such statements because it is clear, quick, and concise.

Expenses common to apartment buildings' operations, including a commentary on each and sources for expense estimates, are discussed later in this chapter.

TERMINOLOGY

Having a grasp of income and expense terminology is fundamental in dealing with any real estate investment. The numbered terms in Exhibit 1-1 (from Case Study 1) all can be defined easily.

1. *Gross income* is the potential annual income the building would bring in if no vacancies or collection loss occurred. *Gross income reflects*

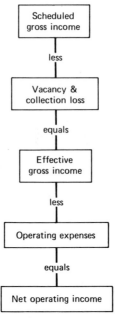

Figure 1-1

no deductions for expenses. Gross income is sometimes called *scheduled gross income* or *potential gross income.*

2.   *Vacancy and collection loss (V&CL)*   is the amount deducted from gross income to account for vacancies and collection losses over the year. The amount depends on the quality of management, tenancy type, rent range, rental housing market, turnover rate, and the economy. Many statements will omit this amount. If this happens, it can be estimated as a percentage of gross income and is usually 1% to 5% in a balanced rental market. If the property is said to experience no vacancies, the rents are probably too low. It is advantageous to a seller to show the vacancy and collection loss as low as possible, so always find out what percentage of the gross income it represents, and make sure that this figure is realistic.

3.   *Effective gross income*   is gross income less the allowance for vacancy and collection loss.

4.   *Fixed expenses*   are the expenses that do not vary according to occupancy. These items would still be paid even if the property were boarded up and vacant.

5.   *Variable expenses*   are those expenses that depend on occupancy

Exhibit 1-1

Income and Expense Schedule
2224 North Wickett Road
Jan, 1, 19＿＿ to Dec. 31, 19＿＿

Income

4 (2-1) @ $300 per month	$ 1,200
8 (1-1) @ $240 per month	1,920
	3,120
	× 12

1. Annual gross income	$37,440	
2. Less: Vacancy and collection loss @ 2%	(749)	
3. Effective gross annual income		$36,691

Expenses

4. Fixed:	
Property taxes	$ 3,750
Insurance	504
5. Variable:	
Gas	592
Electric	175
Water	555
Repairs, maintenance, and decorating	2,568
Gardening	420
Refuse	333
Management @ 2%	734
6. Reserves:	
Stoves (6 @ $240/5 years)	288
Refrigerators (6 @ $250/5 years)	300
Disposals (12 @ $55/5 years)	132
Carpets and drapes (all units/5 years)	1,380

Total expenses	(11,731)
7. Net operating income	$24,960

and management strategy. (Together, fixed and variable expenses are called *operating expenses*.)

6. *Reserves* refers to an expense allowance for the replacement of major short-lived components such as appliances, furniture, carpeting, drapes, roof, water heaters, and other items not allocated in the repairs, maintenance, and decorating category. Since this allowance is future oriented, it will not be found on statements summarizing the past year's expenses, although those items may have been accounted for somewhere in the variable expenses category. Such replacements will fluctuate from year to year, and it is a good procedure to purge any actual replacements from the past statement and replace them with a stabilized annual estimate. Knowing past replacement figures will help us in our estimate, however. The method for estimating reserves and a list of useful life expectancies are discussed later in this chapter.

7. *Net operating income* is effective gross income less the expenses listed above. It *does not* reflect any deductions for loan payments or depreciation allowances. This very important figure is also known as *NOI* or *net income*.

The flow chart in Figure 1-1 shows how these items fit together in arriving at the completed statement.

REVIEWING STATEMENTS

One of the first things the broker or investor must do is review the income and expense statement, not only for the subject property but possibly for other comparable properties as well (to help with the market valuation). The statement often will be incorporated into the broker's set-up sheet or in a multiple listing sheet. Although accuracy and completeness are important, the statements must also be analyzed for consistency. Questions that must be asked are:

Income

1. Does the statement reflect the precise income for the past year, or does it annualize today's rents?
2. If the statement reflects today's rents, are they actual or market (obtainable) rents?
3. Are vacancy and collection losses taken into account?

4. Is concessionary income (laundry, soft drink machines, etc.) taken into account?
5. How accurate are the figures? Are they excessively rounded, indicating guesstimates?

Expenses

1. Is the expense list complete, or does it only include essentials, omitting amounts for service contracts, reserves, and repairs and maintenance?
2. Does the statement reflect a full 12 months of operation?
3. Are the expenses based on actual past experience, or are they projected?
4. Are loan payments, depreciation, or any other improper items included?

There are no set answers or officially designated procedures for some of these questions, but knowing what amount of consistency there is among statements is helpful when analyzing or making value comparisons.

PROJECTING INCOME AND EXPENSES FOR INVESTMENT ANALYSIS

The investment analysis process includes the projection of income and expenses over a proposed holding period. In an inflationary economy, these items can hardly be expected to remain stable. They must be projected to reflect national and local economic expectations as they pertain to the property.

In Case Study 1 the income is assumed to increase at a rate of 8.5% per year, and expenses are assumed to increase at a still faster rate of 12% per year. This represents the analyst's most probable expectation of property performance. A five-year holding period has been chosen with each year's increase based on the previous year's amount resulting in a compounding effect. By convention, *cash flows are considered to be realized at the end of the year (EOY)* with the starting income and expenses based on those experienced at time of purchase. For income, an effective gross figure has been used so that vacancy and collection loss is already taken into account. Example 1-1 is the income and expense projection method used for Case Study 1:

Example 1-1. *Projecting income and expenses.*

The subject property has an effective gross income of $36,691 per year and annual expenses of $11,731 at the time of purchase. Income, *under the most probable expectations,* should increase at the rate of 8.5% per year, whereas expenses are expected to increase at a rate of 12% per year.

Q. What is the net income for each of the next five years based on these expectations?

Income and Expense Growth

End of Year	Income Growth @ 8.5%	Expense Growth @ 12%	Net Income
Start	$36,691	$11,731	$24,960
1	39,810	13,139	26,671
2	43,194	14,716	28,478
3	46,865	16,482	30,383
4	50,849	18,460	32,389
5	55,171	20,675	34,496

EXPENSES

Expenses are deducted from the effective gross income to derive the net operating income. The expense estimate must be adequate to sustain the income projected for the investment.

The importance of expense estimation cannot be emphasized enough. It has been commonplace to estimate expenses as a percentage of the effective gross income or to use the amount proffered in the pro forma. However, using a percentage of gross most often results in too much inaccuracy and is a practice avoided by even the most experienced appraisers and analysts except when making the initial analysis.

Using the set-up sheet or pro forma is a good start; certain information such as utility expenses can be useful. However, these figures must be revised often and the list added to since it is frequently composed of only the very basic expenses. The analysis of expense figures must continue using estimates that reflect the type of management and tenancy the investor plans for the property. Often missing are items such as reserves for replacements, maintenance, and decorating expenses. Also, historical expenses should be given some adjustment for time lag so that the figures reflect current expectations.

The following is a list of expenses often incurred by apartment building operations along with a commentary and list of influencing factors for each. Don't forget to check the rental agreements or leases to see which of the expenses are paid by the landlord.

Property Taxes

Depending on the locality, the property tax may or may not be recomputed upon ownership transfer. In the case of proposed construction, the analyst obtains property tax comparables and correlates an answer by using units of comparison such as assessment per square foot.

Property Insurance

Use will often be made of the premium amount paid for the policy currently on the property since the policy may be transferred along with the change of ownership. However, watch for inadequate coverage due to inflation and the increasing replacement cost. Insurance is usually quoted as a dollar amount for each $1,000 of insurable replacement cost. Lenders may require certain coverages for a particular property such as fire hazard, flood, boiler, or contingent liability insurance. Also, make certain the annual figure used is not the total premium for a three-year policy.

Influencing Factors

Age
Condition
Hazardous conditions
Resident manager
Pool and recreational facilities
Property history—previous claims
Weather
Type construction
Height
Conformity to local or national safety codes
Tenancy type

Utilities

Expense figures for utilities generally can be obtained from the owner or the set-up sheet. Unless your calculations are very complex or detailed guidelines are available, little can be done to determine utility expense estimates independently and accurately due to efficiency variations between properties, services provided, the number of tenants, and so forth.

Influencing Factors

Electricity
   Billing rates and structures
   Number of fixtures
   Types and efficiencies of fixtures
   Type of tenancy
   Master or individually metered
   Style of building
   Amenity and recreational features
Gas
   Number of tenants
   Type of tenancy
   Billing rates and structures
   Appliance efficiency
   Circulating pump for hot water
   Water heater temperature setting
   Master or individually metered
   Amenity and recreational features
Water
   Number of tenants
   Type of tenancy
   Landscape requirements
   Billing rates and structures
   Building efficiency
   Meter accuracy
   Leaks
   Recreational and amenity features

Repairs, Maintenance, and Decorating

This is an expense sometimes omitted on pro formas. However, these amounts can be substantial and should be included in any valuation or analysis. The dollar estimate should be adequate to maintain the property at a level sufficient to sustain the projected gross income. Items in this category can include interior and exterior painting and finishing, janitorial supplies, repairs to plumbing and electrical systems, and the cost of preparing units to rent.

Influencing Factors

    Tenancy type
    Projected rent levels
    Building age
    Building quality
    Condition
    Neighborhood
    Turnover
    Management

Landscaping

This can be taken care of by either a professional gardener or the manager.

Influencing Factors

    Amount of landscaping
    Type of landscaping
    Existing landscape improvements
    Projected rent levels
    Weather
    Soil conditions

Rubbish

Rubbish collection may provided free of charge by the city depending on the locality and size of the property. Commercial collectors commonly use bins of $1\frac{1}{2}$ to 3 cubic yards in size. A 3-cubic-yard bin typically will accommodate up to 12 units with a once a week pickup. A 32-gallon barrel should accommodate a single tenant for a week.

Influencing Factors

    Type of tenancy
    Bin accessibility and Push-out to truck
    Number of tenants
    Custom bin applications
    Time of pickup (routing considerations)

Management

Professional managers usually charge a percentage of the effective gross income for their services. An on-site resident manager may also be needed and is, in fact, required in some localities. Resident manager remuneration often can be estimated according to the number of units in the complex.

Influencing Factors

> Turnover
> Condition
> Size of property
> Tenancy type and demands
> Rental market
> Amount of work in common areas
> Complexity of building systems

Miscellaneous

This category can include termite and pest control, snow removal, city and business licenses, and any other items not accounted for in the other categories.

Service Contracts

Items such as pools, air conditioners, and elevators periodically require servicing by professionals, and this is handled most often on a contract basis. Make sure these expenses aren't budgeted for twice (additional inclusion in the maintenance, repairs, and decorating category).

Influencing Factors

> Pools
>> Pool size
>> Number of people in complex
>> Adequacy and condition of filtering unit
>> Amount and type of landscaping around pool
>> Jacuzzi
>> Exposure to sun
> Elevators
>> Age and condition of equipment

Number of elevators
Number of stops and elevator capacity
Type of mechanical system (hydraulic versus electric)
Type of tenancy
Air conditioning
Climate
Unit exposure to elements
Type of tenancy
Age, quality, and adequacy of system
Type of system

Reserves

An annual reserve amount is calculated by dividing the replacement cost of an item by its useful life. If the item is not expected to be replaced during the holding period, no reserve allowance is taken. Some useful life expectancy guidelines are:

Life Expectancy Guidelines for Reserves*

Item	Estimated Useful Life (Years)
Furniture	2–5
Carpeting	4–8
Drapes	3–5
Roof	12–17
Built-in range and oven	12–15
Freestanding range and oven	10
Refrigerator	7–10
Disposal	3–6
Dishwasher	4–6
Wall air-conditioner	5–9
20–50-gallon water heater	8–10
70–100-gallon water heater	5–10
Hot water circulating pump	10
Pool filter	5
Pool circulating pump	4

*These guidelines should not be relied on for tax computation purposes.

SOURCES FOR EXPENSE ESTIMATES

Sources for estimating operating expenses are limited. If the building is at least one year old, some reliance can be placed on historical expenses. If actual audited statements are not available, the figures lose some credibility. Use can also be made of the operating statements of similar buildings— converting expenses into appropriate common units (such as electric and water costs per square foot and management cost as a percentage of gross) and then applying them to the subject property. Again, the applicability of this method is limited because of the efficiency differences between properties. In cases where contracts or replacement items are involved, it is usually best to go straight to the market and get the costs.

There is only one available publication that deals with apartment building expenses on a national scale. Every year the Institute of Real Estate Management (IREM) publishes a guide for apartment building expense analysis. Entitled *Income/Expense Analysis: Apartments,* * it is a statistical compilation and analysis of actual expenses experienced by apartment building operations. Data submissions are on standardized forms submitted by the Institute's own members, Certified Property Managers. Expenses are separated and presented using two units of comparison: percentage of gross possible total income (%GPTI) and dollars per square foot of rentable area per year ($/square foot)

Each expense is treated with both methods. Data are always presented using at least a median figure and sometimes include a range for each of the two units of comparison (range figures are chosen so that the bottom 25% of the sample falls below the "low" and the top 25% of the sample falls above the "high").

It is obvious that the expenses analyzed using this book should bear a close relationship to either gross income (%GPTI) or square footage ($/square foot.) Such expenses might be management, insurance, repairs, supplies, maintenance, or decorating. Other items such as taxes, landscaping, rubbish removal, and maintenance contracts will need more research.

Income/Expense Analysis: Apartments, Institute of Real Estate Management, Chicago.

CHAPTER TWO

PROPERTY INSPECTION

To assess a property's performance potential properly, it is necessary to inspect the "bricks and mortar"—the part of the investment that actually generates the income stream. This can be done by the broker and investor and may even include the services of a professional property inspector. The professional inspection is generally worth the price and can provide some comfort about the building's condition and weak spots if not prevent the purchase of a lemon.

These vital questions should be kept in mind continually during the inspection:

1. Should the property be producing more income in its present state?
2. What changes to management and/or the property itself might be made to improve the income stream? What will these changes cost?
3. What costs will be incurred in maintaining the property (and income stream)?
4. How management intensive is the property (tenant relations and maintenance)?
5. Is the property well suited to the investor's management and profit philosophies?

Put your creative genius to work in concentrating on possible improvements and their costs. Although maintenance and renovation can be mysterious and intimidating subjects, the purusal of a good home repair book and walks through hardware stores will help familiarize one with job sizes and costs.

RENT ROLL

A copy of the rent roll should be obtained soon after the property gives an indication of having some investment merit. Rent rolls come in all different formats and with varying amounts of information. An example of a good rent roll is given in Exhibit 2-1. It contains enough information to give an indication of the current performance level of the property as well as some insight into the type of tenancy—whether it is a stable group, whether families are involved, and so forth. If a wide price variance exists between units of the same type, this indicates that at least some of the units are at below market rents with a possible opportunity for immediate increases (assuming no rent control). Below market rents will be more common with owner-managed operations than with professional management.

The question of accuracy looms over every rent roll. It would be to the seller's advantage to pad the rent roll, although fear of legal proceedings has been a factor in keeping this practice at a minimum. Rent rolls are generally accurate.

LOCATION

The first items to be considered in the physical inspection are those three important factors of reknown—location, location, and location. The properties immediately adjacent will have the greatest chance of affecting the subject's value. Are they well kept? Are they harmonious in use? Is there anything objectionable about the tenants? Economic theory has long stated the three life cycles of a neighborhood:

1. Growth
2. Stability
3. Decline

Identify which part of the cycle the property is in and at what speed it is moving into the next stage. Strong, growing neighborhoods are the most desirable from the standpoint of aesthetics, but better cash-flow returns can generally be had in the more marginal areas. On the other hand, rent levels and appreciation in declining neighborhoods may not keep pace, so it is a matter of analyzing investment alternatives—precisely the topic that is covered in Part 2 of this book.

The buyer must look at the property from both an owner and tenant's viewpoints. The tenant, who ultimately decides what each apartment will rent for, generally wants a secure location with convenience to transpor-

Exhibit 2-1

Rent Roll
3752 Highland Blvd.
Metropolis
June 1, 1982

Unit Number	Tenant Name	Rooms	Monthly Rent	F/UF	Move-in Date	Delinquency	Number of Persons	Deposit
1	M. Kanis	2/1	$ 300	UF	5-1-74	None	2	$210 LMR*
2	B. Rockwin	2/1	300	UF	12-1-79	None	3	150 SEC†
3	F. Taylor	1/1	240	UF	4-15-81	None	1	150 SEC
4	J. Ethridge	1/1	240	UF	3-1-82	None	2	150 SEC
5	J. Prosser	1/1	240	UF	2-1-79	None	1	150 SEC
6	L. Sanders	1/1	240	UF	5-1-81	None	2	150 SEC
7	N. McKune	2/1	300	UF	11-1-81	None	2	245 LMR
8	R. Sung	2/1	300	UF	9-15-79	None	2	150 SEC
9	D. Armenta	1/1	240	UF	2-1-79	None	2	150 SEC
10	R. Torres	1/1	240	UF	8-1-76	None	1	150 SEC
11	M. Seigler	1/1	240	UF	5-1-77	None	1	180 SEC
12	O. Tapia	1/1	240	UF	7-10-79	None	1	150 SEC

Total Monthly Rent $3,120

* SEC = security deposit.
† LMR = last month's rent.

17

tation, employment, and shopping. Abundant off-site parking for guests may also be desirable. For an owner, pride of ownership will be a consideration as well as location relative to any flood or fire hazard areas. Also, some neighborhoods are designated as civic renewal areas where special low interest rate loans or other inducements may be obtained for renovation. This can be especially appealing.

Always drive around the area surrounding the property and make inquiries regarding vacant units. This not only gives an idea of demand and rent levels but also affords a chance to inquire about what is happening in the neighborhood. An added bonus is that some great buys and listings have been produced this way. Building, zoning, and other municipal officials can be a wealth of knowledge and are some of the few professionals who will talk to you without a fee.

Always investigate. It is surprising how perspectives can change radically after some investigation. When you have a substantial amount of money on the line, there is little excuse for not being well apprised of what is going on.

EXTERIOR INSPECTION

A good deal of information about a building will be known by the time the rent roll is reviewed, the neighborhood is driven through, and the property is seen from the curb. The actual inspection of the property provides a further insight into what creative opportunities may be available and whether a reasonable income can be sustained without excessive expense. Assistance in making the inspection will often be given by a tour leader who may have someone else's best interests in mind—detours sometimes avoid the rough spots. It may be necessary to slow this person down and ask that attention be given to spots bypassed. You will look more seasoned, and the leader most often will be gracious and cooperative, even if a problem is uncovered. Following are questions that should be answered in the investigation of the exterior—the part that can be seen without gaining access to the unit interiors:

Landscaping

1. How much landscape maintenance is required?
2. Is there drainage away from the building and parking area into a sewer system (not onto another property unless a drainage easement exists)?
3. Are there built-in sprinklers?

4. Are the trees deciduous? Does their nearness to any pool create a problem?
5. Can immediate improvements be made by trimming and watering?
6. Is there a resident manager who can handle the landscaping chores?
7. If there is a landscape service, how often does it visit the property?
8. Do the grounds reflect pride on the part of the tenants?

Driveway and Parking

1. How many parking spaces exist? How many per unit? Are there enough spaces to accommodate a possible condo conversion?
2. Is there an adequate turnaround area?
3. Are there oil spots on the pavement?
4. Are any support posts or walls damaged?
5. If there is a parking gate, is it operational? Is it operated by a card or a key? If key operated, does it use the unit entry key?
6. If parking is enclosed and covered, is there adequate ventilation? Fire sprinklers?
7. Are there any cracks or holes in the pavement?

Lighting

1. Is there adequate exterior lighting?
2. Is the lighting incandescent or fluorescent?
3. Are the lights on automatic timers?
4. Is the exterior lighting wired to the tenants' meters or to the landlord's?
5. Do the lights noticeably enhance the appearance of the property at night and provide adequate security?
6. Should more lighting be added?

Exterior Walls

1. Are the materials appropriate for the location and climate?
2. What amount of repair work is needed?
3. What condition is the paint in? What preparation work will be required for the next painting?
4. Are the screens in place?
5. Are the gutters and downspouts complete and in good repair?

6. Has the window sash finish streaked onto the walls?
7. What condition is the trim in?

Roof

Roof condition is especially important, not only because of replacement cost but also because of possible water damage to unit interiors and tenants' possessions. Any building over two stories high should have stairway access to the roof. Always inspect it.

Most apartment buildings have roofs that are flat or appear to be, but should actually have a slope of at least ¼ inch per foot to accommodate runoff and prevent ponding. It is impossible to make a thorough inspection of a roof from only the exterior surface since a pinhole can leak enough to create extensive damage. Also, the roof may have air conditioning, ventilation, or elevator equipment mountings whose connections enter through the roof and can cause problems. Try to gain interior access to some of the top floor units where any leakage may be evident.

1. How old is the roof? What is its remaining life expectancy?
2. Has it received the trial of at least a few hard rains?
3. Of what material is the roofing?
4. Does the roof carry a warranty? Is it transferable?
5. Are the drainage provisions adequate? Are they functional?

Laundry Room

1. Is the laundry room attractive and in good repair?
2. Who owns the machines? What is the income?
3. What condition are the walls and ceiling in?
4. Does the room reflect pride and consideration on the part of the tenants?

Recreation Room

1. What condition are the walls and ceiling in?
2. Is there removable personal property that may have to be replaced due to theft?
3. Are there appliances? Are they in good working order?
4. Is the room available on a full-time, limited-time, or reservation basis?
5. What income is received from any concession machines?

6. What additional management burden will be created by the recreation room?

Elevators

Any building over two stories high generally has at least one elevator. Buildings from two to four stories most often have a hydraulic elevator that operates by oil pumped into and out of a plunger unit, much the same as a grease rack in a service station bay. The mechanics for this type of installation are located adjacent to the bottom of the shaft. Hydraulic elevators cost substantially less to maintain than electric elevators that are more suitable for building heights over 60 feet requiring five or more stops. Doors, controls, and other cab appointments can be identical in both types of elevators.

The elevator should have a service contract that can be a preventive maintenance or, preferably, a full service (including labor and parts) agreement. The maintenance expense of operating two elevators placed adjacent to each other might run 20% higher due to added complications in the mechanical system. The complexities of the elevator shaft and mechanics make a thorough inspection practically impossible, but they should still be looked at for any obvious problems.

Pool

1. Is it heated? How many months is the heat generally left on?
2. Does the filter system appear to be in good repair? Is the water clean?
3. Does the pool surface need repair or an acid wash?
4. Has the pool been adequately maintained?
5. Are the proper warnings to swimmers in place?
6. Is the pool fenced?
7. Is there adequate furniture?
8. Is the pool surface or deck cracked?

Entry

1. Is the entry attractive? What can be done to enhance it inexpensively?
2. What condition are the mail boxes in?
3. Are the handrails sturdy?
4. Are there security systems? Do they work properly?

Utility Meters

1. Are the units individually metered for gas and electricity?
2. Are the meters protected from possible auto damage?

Stairs and Decks

1. Have the stairs and decks been maintained continually to prevent waterlogging of substructures?
2. Are the handrails sturdy, safe, and well finished?

Rubbish Area

1. Is the rubbish area well shielded?
2. Is it conveniently located for both tenants and the disposal service?
3. Is there adequate space and capacity?
4. If bins are used, are they on a concrete pad (asphalt can be destroyed quickly)?
5. Can the area be cleaned easily?

Plumbing

The water heater is often taken for granted but may be suffering from a lack of maintenance. Water heaters should be drained once or twice a year to remove any sediments that collect on the bottom, harden, and insulate the water from the flame. These deposits can become several inches thick. A large central heater may have a door at the bottom where sediment can be cleaned out. The operating capacity of a water heater will be given on a tag on its side and is measured in number of gallons and BTU output. Check to see if the system has a water softener, filter, purifier, or chemical feeder. Although the installation of such devices implies that they are necessary, they can be costly to maintain and operate.

Copper plumbing is an excellent material except in areas where the water is particularly hard causing mineral deposits in the pipes.

INTERIOR INSPECTION

A seller typically will want some evidence of intent on the part of the purchasing party before disturbing the occupants and raising suspicions about rent raises or evictions. Only a few units are generally accessible for inspection, and whether those inspected are truly representative of the building will remain a mystery until after the purchase. Ask to see at least one of each type of unit with at least one on the top floor so that any roof leak and its accompanying damage might be detected. Make sure the rent roll agrees in room count with those units observed during the inspection.

Flooring

1. What is the condition, style, and quality?
2. Is it attractive?
3. How much life is left before replacement?
4. Will it coordinate with a variety of furnishing tastes?
5. Does the carpet have nonremovable stains or odors?

Walls and Ceilings

1. Are the walls strong or flimsy?
2. What amount of damage is there? How much of it is beyond simple patch-up repair?
3. Are the colors pleasant?
4. Will these walls be repainted at the next renting?
5. Are there adequate electric outlets and lighting fixtures?
6. Are there adequate closets in the right places?
7. Is there an intercom system or TV master antenna? Does the intercom work?

Doors and Windows

1. Do the doors and windows open freely? Sticky windows and doors may be a sign of foundation settlement.
2. Do they provide adequate ventilation?

Fireplace

1. Does it have an artifical gas log?
2. If it doesn't, does the flue work properly?

Security

1. Do the doors have adequate locks?
2. Do the windows offer prime spots for unwanted entry?

Electrical Fixtures

1. What fixtures need replacement?
2. Can the addition of any new fixtures greatly enhance the appeal of the unit?

Air-Conditioning

1. What type is it? Wall? Window? Forced air?
2. Is it adequate for the entire apartment or just one room?
3. Are any parts missing?
4. Will it need servicing? How often?
5. Does the system require a service contract? Such a contract usually includes filter replacement, lubrication, condenser cleaning, and compression switch and compressor motor inspection.

Heat

1. What type of heating system does the building have? Is it floor, wall, radiant, steam, gravity, or forced air?
2. If there is a boiler, how often has it been inspected?
3. How old is the boiler? Will it need replacing soon?
4. Does the system evidence any leaks or disrepair?
5. Is any gas heating system properly ventilated?
6. Is there a thermostat?
7. Is the system working properly?

Kitchen

1. Is there adequate ventilation?
2. Do the appliances belong to the building? If so, do they work and are they stylish? Are any refrigerators missing interior pieces?
3. Does the disposal work?
4. Is there enough lighting?
5. Does the exhaust fan motor work? Is it noisy, evidencing need of repair or replacement?
6. What is the style and condition of the faucets?
7. Are there adequate cabinets, countertops, and cupboards?
8. What is the condition of the countertops?
9. Does the sink have any nonremovable stains?

Bathroom

1. Is there any water damage or signs of plumbing leaks?
2. Look under the sink. What materials is the plumbing made of?
3. Is there adequate storage?
4. Is the mirror in need of replacement?
5. Are there any nonremovable stains on the fixtures?
6. What kind of enclosure does the shower have?
7. If there is a sliding glass door, does it operate properly?
8. Is there adequate ventilation? If there is a fan, does it rattle or make excessive noise?
9. Look at the underside of the toilet tank lid to check the building age. The date the property was built may be stamped here.
10. Are there any dry rot or fungus infestations?
11. Do the shower and sink drain properly? Is the water pressure satisfactory?

CHAPTER THREE

THE VALUATION PROCESS

Different values can exist for the same property: assessed value, insurable value, and so forth. However, we are most interested in *market value:*

> The highest price in terms of money which a property will bring in a competitive and open market under all conditions requisite to a fair sale, the buyer and seller, each acting prudently, knowledgeably and assuming the price is not affected by undue stimulation.*

Market value is estimated by analyzing sales and listings of similar properties. Units of comparison are *abstracted* from other sales, and these *value indicators* are applied to the property being valued. The sales that are analyzed are called *comparable sales* or *comparables,* and the property being valued is the *subject property.*

ECONOMIC AND PHYSICAL APPROACHES

The comparative methods of valuation most applicable for brokers and investors are:

Economic Methods

1. Gross rent multiplier (GRM)
2. Overall rate (OAR)

*Boyce, Byrl N. (Ed.), American Institute of Real Estate Appraisers, Society of Real Estate Appraisers (sponsors), *Real Estate Appraisal Terminology,* Ballinger Publishing Company, Cambridge, MA, 1975, p. 137.

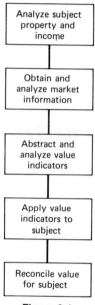

Figure 3-1

Physical Methods

    1.   Dollars per room

    2.   Dollars per unit

    3.   Dollars per square foot

Another approach, gaining favor because of its ability to account directly for tax consequences as well as income and value increases, is the "present value" technique. This more complex technique is discussed in Chapter 11.

Of the two methods listed here, the *economic* indicators are usually favored since they are associated with the investor's primary concern: income.

The physical approaches deal with the building—the physical means for producing this income—and are more removed from what really constitutes value. Therefore, when physical methods are used, the comparables should have a similar earning potential for the unit of comparison.

At least several approaches should be applied and a final value *reconciled* from all these value indications with the *proper emphasis given each according to its applicability and reliability*. This reconciliation process is a mental judgment and *not* a mathematical averaging.

STEPS IN THE VALUATION PROCESS

1. Obtain the subject property's income and expense statement for the current year as well as the last three years if possible.
2. Find comparable properties for which reliable and pertinent sales, listings, and/or income data are obtainable.
3. Investigate the nature of each sale, including sale price, financing, and, if possible, where income was in relation to the obtainable market level at that time.
4. Analyze the important attributes of each sale in relation to the corresponding attributes of the property being valued.
5. Abstract the necessary information from the comparables and apply to the subject those valuation approaches deemed applicable and for which reliable information is available.
6. Consider the reliability of the data and the applicability of each approach, and use your best judgment in reconciling the value indications into a final estimate of value. This estimate should be rounded to at least the nearest $1,000 so you do not imply an improbable degree of accuracy.

VALUE FACTORS

Each method for obtaining a value indicator involves the abstraction and division of two numbers from each comparable sale:

Value Indicator	Abstraction from Comparables
Gross rent multiplier	$\dfrac{\text{sale price}}{\text{gross income}}$
Capitalization with an overall rate	$\dfrac{\text{net income}}{\text{sale price}}$
Dollars per room	$\dfrac{\text{sale price}}{\text{number of rooms}}$
Dollars per unit	$\dfrac{\text{sale price}}{\text{number of units}}$
Dollars per square foot	$\dfrac{\text{sale price}}{\text{number of square feet}}$

Sale price is common to all approaches. After the sale price is ascertained, one more item is acquired for each of the approaches used. Whereas sale price is usually a rather imponderable figure not subject to differing interpretations, the other items (income and physical units) are more vulnerable to erroneous reporting, misinterpretation, and varying methods of measurement. Careful research to ensure accuracy and the use of common standards of measurement are important. After being abstracted, the indicators are applied to the appropriate income or physical measurement of the subject to derive an estimate of value.

SALE PRICE AND VALUE

Note that in the discussions to follow, the term *sale price always refers to a comparable sale,* and the term *value always refers to the subject property* for which we are estimating value.

Sale price and value are not synonymous terms—sale prices of comparables occasionally fluctuate from their market value due to nepotism, duress, and so forth. However, barring any evidence to the contrary, assume that the sale price of the comparable reflects the fair market value so that comparisons can be made. Also, note that we continually use the term estimating value. It would be presumpuous to say that we are determining value and erroneous to say that we are producing value.

USING LISTINGS

Listings are an excellent aid to estimating value. Most of the information required to apply the various valuation approaches is readily available and reflects the current market. Listings are limited to indicating the top end of the range since the listing prices are usually subject to some negotiation.

SALE PRICE FLUCTUATIONS

Since the value indicators are taken from market sales, the perfect working climate for their abstraction and application would require a market that bears a constant, nonfluctuating relationship between sale price and the corresponding income or physical units used in the comparison. If this were the case, only a single comparable would be needed, and estimating value would become the simplest of sciences. However, this is not the case.

Abstracting value indicators from comparable sales and then applying them to a specific property is a process based on surface figures: sale price and the respective income or physical units. An inherent presumption made in using comparable sales is that sale price and value maintain a direct relationship to the units of comparison—that value can be estimated purely on income, purely on room count, or on a similar basis. This presumption is erroneous because of the numerous considerations beyond the building's income or physical condition that the purchaser may have made in formulating what to pay for the property. Each transaction has impacts that are peculiar only to it, resulting in biased value indicators. Adjustments for these differences are often based on a "gut feeling" and are reflected in the final choice of the value indicator after close consideration of the impacts involved in each comparable sale and how each impact relates to the corresponding factor of the subject property. Impacts that must be considered when abstracting or applying value indicators are as follows:

1. *Expense Ratio.* Valuation methods other than capitalization of net income with an OAR assume that a constant portion of the gross income of each property is attributable to expenses. This is seldom the case since a number of expenses are involved, and each expense is in turn affected by its own influencing factors.

2. *Market Rents.* For the economic methods to work properly, rents for the subject and comparable sales must be at the market level or else bear a consistent relationship to it so that fair comparisons can be made. The historic nature of the comparables may make it impossible to go back in time and adjust their rents to the historic level or even to tell whether their rents were at the market level to start with. If the comparables' rents were below market value at the time of sale, a high sale price may have been paid based on the prospect of raising the rents, resulting in an artificially high value indicator. Adjusting the subject rents to the going market level and then applying an economic-based unit of comparison computed from comparables that may not have had their rents at the market level at the time of sale can be an error-prone process.

3. *Financing.* The comparison process loses effectiveness as the variations and importance of financing continue to grow. Indicators can carry misleading assumptions of similar interest rates, loan-to-value ratios, and equity investment. Also, abstracting indicators from transactions where tax deferred exchanges, assumptions, or installment sales were used is risky and sometimes inadvisable unless the subject property financing is apt to be similarly structured.

4. *Time of Sale.* The time/value relationship is often considered self-adjusting in the economic methods due to the corresponding changes in income. This is true to a certain extent although a steady relationship rarely

exists. The physical methods do not take time into account at all, so some inflationary or deflationary adjustment of the indicator may be necessary.

5. *Condition.* Condition also is often considered to be self-adjusting in the economic methods in that the tenant theoretically adjusts the rent accordingly. However, the tenant would confine this adjustment to observable conditions and would probably not include such items as roof condition, mechanical systems, and so forth. Also, a premium may be paid by a purchaser for an especially clean property purely because of the appeal to pride of ownership. Condition differences are not considered in the physical methods, so some adjustments again may be necessary.

6. *Depreciation.* The value indicators do not recognize depreciation advantages that occur with the varying land-to-improvement ratios.

7. *Buyer's Motivations.* The sale price for a particular property may be distorted because of influences such as proximity to the buyer's other properties and residence. Also, when valuing properties with owner's units, it is best to use comparables that also have this amenity.

8. *Seller's Motivations.* A price other than fair market value may be taken due to duress, nepotism, illness, divorce, and so forth.

9. *Lack of Market Knowledge.* Transactions in which the buyer or seller acts with insufficient sophistication or market information may have sale prices not reflecting the market value of the property.

10. *Furnished Versus Unfurnished.* A furnished building caters to a more transient tenant and requires more management, expense, and investment than the unfurnished building does. The additional tenant turnover will probably mean more vacancy loss (although a fast turnover may be advantageous in a rent-control situation if the rents can be raised for new tenants). Also, additional tax shelter is provided by the quicker depreciation allowed on personal property.

11. *Future Influences.* Possibilities of future condemnation, rent control, or encroaching influences are not always subject to equal consideration between sales.

12. *Age.* Older buildings are usually bought with lower value indicators compared to newer buildings in the same area.

13. *Size.* The value indicators tend to decrease as the property gets larger. Comparing properties of different sizes may well result in biased indicators.

This list demonstrates the vulnerability of the different approaches, but these impacts can be minimized by proper selection and research of the comparables. This coupled with good judgment will serve to reinforce the reliability of each approach.

CHAPTER FOUR

VALUATION APPROACHES

GROSS RENT MULTIPLIER

The easiest and most frequently used method for valuing apartment buildings is the *gross rent multiplier* (GRM). The GRM is a number abstracted from comparable sales which then multiplies the gross income of the subject into an estimate of value:

$$\text{GRM} \times \text{gross income} = \text{value estimate}$$

Gross income is the income generated by the property without any deductions for expenses. Further, the gross income is usually the entire scheduled gross income (as opposed to effective gross income, which includes an allowance for vacancy and collection loss).

Annual or Monthly GRMs

Gross rent multipliers may be abstracted and applied to either annual or monthly income. The monthly multiplier is always 12 times the annual multiplier. The annual multiplier has gained the greatest popularity and is usually carried to one decimal place (8.8, 9.5, etc.). Carrying the number to more decimal places implies a degree of accuracy that does not usually exist in the valuation process.

Abstracting the GRM

Dividing the sales price of a comparable sale by its gross income results in the gross rent multiplier indicated for that specific sale:

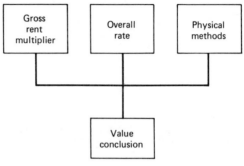

Figure 4-1

Example 4-1. *Abstracting the GRM from a comparable sale.*
In researching the market, a comparable is found that was sold for $1,000,000 and had a gross income of $121,950.

Q. By the process of abstraction, what is the GRM?

A. $\text{GRM} = \dfrac{\text{sale price}}{\text{gross income}} = \dfrac{\$1,000,000}{\$121,950} = 8.2$

Applying the GRM

The GRM's application to the subject property is the reverse operation of abstracting it:

Example 4-2. *Applying the gross rent multiplier.*
A research of the market uncovers sales with GRMs of 7.9, 7.9, 8.0, 8.2, and 8.7. After researching the properties and circumstances behind the sales, a GRM of 8.1 is chosen to be applied to the subject property. The subject has an annual gross income of $110,000.

Q. What is the value estimate for the subject using the 8.1 GRM?

A. 8.1 × $110,000 = $891,000
        Round to: $890,000

OVERALL RATE

Efficiencies of building operations differ as to what services are furnished, the layout, age, physical structure, amount of maintenance work, and location. Since the efficiencies of operation vary between comparables and subject, there exists a need for a valuation method that accounts for the accompanying fluctuation of expenses.

It is possible to account for expense variations simply by measuring value as a function of net income rather than gross income. The method that does this is called the capitalization approach. In this approach, an *overall rate* (OAR) is applied to the *net income* to arrive at the value estimate.

Capitalization actually means the conversion of an income stream into an estimate of value which explains the often used term, capitalizing income.

Abstracting the Overall Rate

The overall rate is abstracted from a comparable sale by dividing net income by sale price:

Example 4-3. *Abstracting an OAR from a market sale.*
A comparable is found that was sold for $1,000,000 and had a net income of $86,000.

Q. By the process of abstraction, what is the overall rate?

A. $\text{OAR} = \dfrac{\text{net income}}{\text{sale price}} = \dfrac{\$86,000}{\$1,000,000} = 0.086 \text{ or } 8.6\%$

Besides considering expenses, there is one additional difference between the direct capitalization and rent multiplier methods: The OAR is always expressed as a percentage rather than a whole number: Instead of income divided into sale price to abstract the OAR, sale price is divided into income, resulting in a decimal. This helps avoid possible confusion about whether a particular number is an OAR or a GRM.

Applying the OAR

Once a number of sales are researched and a rate selected, the OAR is divided into the net income of the subject property, which gives us a value estimate:

Example 4-4. *Applying the overall rate to the subject property.*
The subject property has a current net income of $79,000. The OAR abstracted from the market sales is 8.8%.

Q. Applying the overall rate to the net income of the subject property, what is the estimate of value?

A. Value estimate $= \dfrac{\text{net income}}{\text{OAR}} = \dfrac{\$79,000}{0.088} = \$897,727$

    Round to: $900,000

The OAR/Value Relationship

The overall rate is a rate of return. It is the percentage of sale price or value that is received annually as net income. Conversely, value can be measured according to the net income produced by the property.

The buyer in the last example valued the property based on a net income stream that was 8.8% of what the purchase price was to be (see Figure 4-2).

Had more risk and management and less liquidity and pride of ownership been involved, the buyer most probably would require a greater net income-to-value ratio (higher OAR) to offset these disadvantages. On the other hand, with less risk and more liquidity, the investor would probably settle for a smaller income stream in relation to purchase price, resulting in a lower OAR. The OAR bears an inverse relationship to value: the higher the OAR, the lower the value estimate. A detailed discussion of how risk, liquidity, and management affect rates of return can be found in Chapter 12.

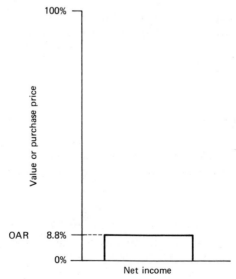

Figure 4-2. Net income/oar relationship.

Reliability and Variations of Expenses

The capitalization method's superior edge over the gross rent multiplier approach is in its ability to account for operating efficiency differences between properties. The less accuracy in the expense figures of the comparables and subject, the more this advantage is diluted. The expense figures can be biased or inaccurate for any of the following reasons:

Different accounting methods.

Exclusion of reserve allowances on the income and expense statement.

Inclusion of personal expenses not directly attributable to the operation of the property itself.

An atypical year for property expenses due to improvements or renovation. Proper distinctions must be made not to include any capital improvements.

Inaccurate figures.

Expenses not reflective of a full 12-month period.

If, due to any of these reasons, the expense figures are insufficient, the investor or broker may rely more on the GRM or physical methods.

BAND OF INVESTMENT

Based on a knowledge of the investor's expectations for the return on the equity investment as well as certain terms of the available financing, one can *construct* an overall rate. This technique is of most benefit to buyers who wish to make a purchase based on a certain cash return, but it can also be used by the seller in estimating value.

The required variables for construction of an overall rate through the band of investment technique are:

Loan-to-value ratio (as a percentage).

Equity-to-value ratio (as a percentage).

Annual loan constant (the annual payments as a percentage of the loan amount).

The investor's expected cash flow rate (annual before-tax return required by the investor on the equity invesment).

Loan and Equity Ratios

The loan-to-value ratio on available financing is often a matter of common knowledge or should be available from the lender in cases where new financing of the property is sought.

Equity is the purchaser's cash contribution to the purchase price exclusive of closing costs. *The equity-to-value ratio is the ratio of this payment to the value or purchase price.*

Because purchase price is composed of loan and equity, their ratios together will total 100%: if the loan-to-value ratio is 65%, then the equity-to-value ratio is 35%.

Annual Constant

The annual loan constant is the percentage of the loan amount paid by the borrower to the lender in annual payments. It is calculated by dividing the loan amount into the annual loan payment. However, at this juncture the value and the loan amount may not be known. The constant may still be found by dividing any loan amount* by its *annual* payment figured at the particular loan term and interest rate.

Cash-Flow Rate

The remainder of the net operating income (NOI), now that expenses and loan payment have been allocated, is the *cash flow* or equity dividend to the investor. The investor has an expectation or requirement of this annual amount, and this expectancy or demand is expressed as a percentage of the equity investment. This is called the *cash-flow rate (CFR), cash-on-cash return,* or *equity-dividend rate.* Continuing with the previous example, assume that an annual return on cash-flow rate of 4% is expected on the 35% equity position (see Figure 4-3). (This rate can be abstracted from the market and is demonstrated in Example 4-7.)

The cash-flow rate may appear outwardly to be a rather low rate of return on the cash investment, but, as can be seen in the analysis section of this book, the CFR is only the first year, before-tax cash return on the equity investment, and the investor is relying on the true rate of return to be enhanced by increasing income, tax shelter, and equity growth.

To apply the band of investment technique, consider the case of a property on which a purchaser is considering making an offer based on a 12% per annum interest, 30-year, 65% loan. To find the annual constant, the loan amount can be set arbitrarily at $100,000, resulting in a monthly payment

---

*When using the financial calculator to find the constant, use Calculator Procedure 1, and set the loan amount at 1. This will automatically provide a percentile monthly figure, which is multiplied by 12 to obtain the annual constant.

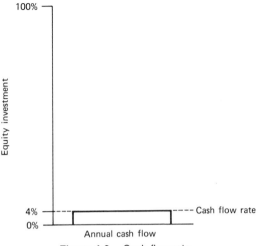

Figure 4-3. Cash-flow rate.

of $1,018.43, and giving us an annual payment of $12,221.16. Dividing this annual payment by the $100,000 loan amount results in 0.1222, the annual constant (see Figure 4-4).

$$\text{Annual constant} = \frac{\text{loan payment}}{\text{loan amount}} = \frac{\$12,221.16}{\$100,000} = 0.1222$$

Combining Loan and Equity

Whatever the value is, 0.1222 of 65% of that value is going to be paid in loan payments, and 35% of the value is expected to yield a 4% return on the investor's equity. Combining the above loan/equity parameters gives us our overall rate:

Example 4-5. *Constructing an OAR through the band of investment.*
Assume the following loan and equity parameters:

(a) Loan-to-value ratio of 65% and a 0.1222 annual loan constant.
(b) Equity-to-value ratio of 35% and a 4% cash-flow rate.

Q. Using the band of investment technique, what is the overall rate?

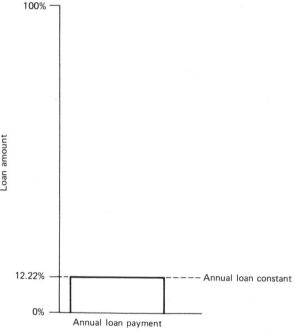

Figure 4-4. Annual loan constant.

A.

L-to-V ratio	×	ac	=	0.65	×	0.1222	=	0.0794
E-to-V ratio	×	edr	=	0.35	×	0.04	=	0.0140
Overall rate							=	0.0934

Dividing the OAR into the NOI (for instance, $70,000) gives an estimate of value for the property:

$$\text{Value} = \frac{\text{NOI}}{\text{OAR}} = \frac{\$70,000}{0.0934} = \$749,465$$

Round to: $750,000

The band of investment technique really calculates what percentage of the value the NOI must be to satisfy loan payments and equity return (cash-flow rate) requirements. Given the NOI, the value can then be estimated.

More than One Loan

If more than one loan is involved, it is merely added to the band of investment:

Example 4-6.   *Building an OAR with a second loan involved.*

Assume that along with the 65% first loan, the seller takes back a second loan for 10% of the value payable at 10% per annum interest only. The equity position is now only 15%, but the expected equity dividend rate is still 4%.

Q.   Using the band of investment technique, what is the overall rate?

A.   First loan: 0.65×0.1222 =   0.0794
    Second loan: 0.10×0.10 =   0.0100
    Equity: 0.15×0.04 =   0.0060
    Overall rate   =   0.0954

Abstracting the Cash-Flow Rate

The band of investment produces more of an estimate of investment value than market value since it is based on the annual equity return expected by one particular investor rather than on the market as a whole. However, by abstracting the cash-flow rate from the market (other sales), we once again approach the concept of estimating market value.

The cash-flow rate can be abstracted from a comparable sale by finding the dollar amount of equity investment and dividing it into the annual cash flow provided by that property. This is illustrated by reversing example 4-6.

Example 4-7.   *Abstracting a cash-flow rate.*

An apartment building with a net income of $70,000 is sold for $750,000. A 65% loan was obtained that had an annual loan payment of $59,578.

Q.   What is the cash-flow rate?
A.   First, figure the equity investment:

> Total price $750,000
> Equity Ratio $\times$ 0.35
> Equity amount $262,500

Second, the cash flow is found by subtracting the annual loan payment from the NOI:

> NOI $70,000
> Annual loan payment   (59,578)
> Cash flow $10,422

Third, the cash-flow rate is found by *dividing the equity investment into the cash flow:*

$$\text{Cash-flow rate} = \frac{\$10,422}{\$262,500} = 4\%$$

When a figure is obtained for the market cash-flow rate, it can be inserted into the band of investment model and the market overall rate can be synthesized.

PHYSICAL METHODS OF COMPARISON

Physical methods of comparison generally are given secondary emphasis in making value estimates. Because the apartment building itself is really a material means to obtain an income stream, value is more dependent on income expectations, and more emphasis is usually placed on the economic methods of finding value. However, physical methods are often good indicators that can be used in addition to the economic approaches and are especially helpful when reliable income information is difficult to obtain. All the information needed to apply the physical methods may be on file at a county assessor's office. The physical methods covered here are:

Physical Valuation Methods

1. Dollars per room
2. Dollars per unit
3. Dollars per square foot

The properties compared should have similar income-producing capabilities based on the particular unit of comparison. Some adjustment may be desirable to compensate for income variations—appropriate techniques are discussed in the Adjusting Comparables section of this chapter. In general, the properties should also:

Be in similar locations
Be of similar age, style, and quality
Be of similar size
Have similar unit mixes

In addition, all of the hazards examined in the previous chapter (Sale Price Fluctuations) must be considered.

Dollars per Room

As the name implies, this method divides the sale price of a comparable sale by the number of its rooms. Consistency is again a key since a common standard must be used to define what should be counted as a room. No universal standard exists, although living rooms, bedrooms, kitchens, and sometimes bathrooms are counted as separate rooms. Dining areas are sometimes given the status of one-half room, but dining rooms are usually considered full rooms.

Exhibit 4-1. Dollars per Room

Abstraction from Comparable	Application to Subject
$/room $= \dfrac{\text{sale price}}{\text{number of rooms}}$	Value estimate = number of rooms × $/room

Dollars per Unit

This method can be thought of as a less refined version of dollars per room. Its use depends on the buildings under comparison having similar rent potentials per unit. For instance, a building with all one-bedroom units should not be compared to a building having two- and three-bedroom units.

Exhibit 4-2. Dollars per Unit

Abstraction from Comparable	Application to Subject
$/unit $= \dfrac{\text{sale price}}{\text{number of units}}$	Value estimate = number of units × $/unit

Dollars per Square Foot

Square footage counts must be accurate and be based on a mutual standard of measurement. The *gross* area of a building (exclusive of walkways and parking areas) generally is used. Square footage measurement sometimes can be found at the assessor's office or in the building department of the city.

Exhibit 4-3. Dollars per Square Foot

Abstraction from Comparable	Application to Subject
$/square foot $= \dfrac{\text{sale price}}{\text{number of square feet}}$	Value estimate = number of square feet × $/square foot

Examples

The following are examples of abstracting the three physical value indicators from a comparable and then applying a final reconciled value indicator to the subject property. These indicators, in addition to those found in any of the economic approaches used, are reconciled into a final estimate of value.

Example 4-8. *Abstracting physical units of comparison.*
A comparable is found that sold for $600,000. Pertinent specifications of the building are:

(a) 89 rooms
(b) 25 units
(c) 16,850 square feet

Q. By abstraction, what are the three physical value indicators?

A. *Dollars per Room*
$/room $= \dfrac{\text{sale price}}{\text{number of rooms}} = \dfrac{\$600{,}000}{89} = \$\ 6{,}742$

Dollars per unit
$/unit $= \dfrac{\text{sale price}}{\text{number of units}} = \dfrac{\$600{,}000}{25} = \$24{,}000$

Dollars per square foot
$/square foot $= \dfrac{\text{sale price}}{\text{number of square feet}} = \dfrac{\$600{,}000}{16{,}850} = \$35.61$

Example 4-9. *Applying the physical value indicators.*
After abstracting the physical indicators from the comparable in the previous example and from several others, you have reconciled the following value indicators:

Dollars per room	$6,800
Dollars per unit	$24,500
Dollars per square foot	$36.00

The subject property has 74 rooms, 21 units, and 124,300 square feet.

Q. What are the respective indications of value using these three value indicators?

A. *Dollars per Room*

Value estimate = $/room × number of rooms = $6,800 × 74 = $503,200

Dollars per Unit

Value estimate = $/unit × number of units = $24,500 × 21 = $514,500

Dollars per Square Foot

Value estimate = $/square foot × number of square feet = $36.00 × 14,300 = $514,800

ADJUSTING COMPARABLES

There are two main types of comparables: comparable sales used in valuating the subject property and comparable rents that indicate whether the subject's rents are in line with the current rental market. Both kinds of comparables ideally would be obtained from identical properties located on the same block. However, there are almost always substantial differences between the comparables and the subject, some of which must be adjusted if a fair comparison is to be made. One way of dealing with these differences is to obtain enough comparables that, blended with good judgement, will provide a reasonably good indicator. However, it is sometimes desirable to use more refined methods.

Adjusting Rent Comparables

Market rentals vary not only between different buildings but between units within the same building as well. Some of the reasons for these rent differences are as follows:

1. Unit size, or number of rooms.
2. Building quality, condition, and age.
3. Building amenities.
4. Furnished versus unfurnished.
5. Appliances provided by landlord versus tenant.
6. Utilities paid for by landlord versus tenant.
7. Air-conditioning.
8. Patios and balconies.
9. Views.

10. Parking.
11. Lease terms, deposits, and fees.
12. Built-in appliances.

Depending on the item, adjustments can be made in different ways. For example, the subject property may provide refrigerators for each unit, whereas the units being matched against the subject for rent comparison purposes do not. Although a refrigerator could be rented from a third party (rental store) for $30 a month, the cost of the same refrigerator might be $400. If the landlord were to purchase and include this refrigerator with the rent, the cost amortized over a 10-year life would be $4.00 per month. However, some additional consideration would be required by the landlord to compensate for risk, financing charges, profit, and so forth. Interviews with several property managers in the area might suggest that the inclusion of a refrigerator with an apartment might command an additional $10.00 a month in rent. After a consideration of the findings—cost to provide the refrigerator as well as interviews with those familiar with the market—one may conclude that the additional rent created by the refrigerator is indeed $10.00 per month. Thus if the otherwise identical unit next door rents for $320 without a refrigerator, the subject unit with a refrigerator should rent for $330. More often, adjustments will be made for several items. Exhibit 4-4 is an example of a rent adjustment grid that might be found in the report of a professional appraiser.

Exhibit 4-4. One-Bedroom Rent Comparable Adjustments and Correlation

Item	Subject	Comparable 1 1052 Franklin	Comparable 2 948 Franklin	Comparable 3 1112 Hightower
Current rent	$340	$340	$330	$355
Refrigerator	Yes	No	Yes	Yes
		+$10	—	—
Parking	Covered	Covered	None	Uncovered
		—	+$15	+$5
Sauna	No	No	No	Yes
		—	—	−$5
Condition	Average	Average	Fair	Very good
		—	+$10	−$15
Total adjustments		+$10	+$25	−$15
Indicated rent*		$350	$355	$340

*Indicated market rental for subject property one-bedroom units is $350.

In arriving at the final conclusion, weighted emphasis generally is given according to number and size of adjustments. In Exhibit 4-4, 1052 Franklin Avenue appears to be the best comparable and is listed as comparable 1. Perhaps the best indicator is the subject itself, and some thought should be given to how closely $340 reflects the current market rent. The indicated market rent generally is chosen from the high end of the range since the low end may indicate that the comparables themselves deviate from the market.

Adjusting Comparable Sales

Although it is common to adjust rent to market level, the practice of adjusting value indicators of comparable sales has generated more critical comment and is usually carried out only after a thorough search of comparable sales turns up insufficient data. Before adjusting the indicators for the various units of comparison, it is necessary to know whether the differences are compensated for in the value indicator used. For instance, although a difference in unit interior conditions between the subject and comparable may necessitate some adjustment in the dollar per unit or dollar per square foot indicator, the difference would probably be self-compensating in the income approaches because of the differences in rent. Time of sale may be similarly self-adjusting in the income approaches with increased rents acting as the compensating factor. The physical approaches are not self-adjusting for time, however, and some factoring using the rate of property value appreciation (or depreciation) may be necessary.

Adjusting the Physical Indicators

A pure application of the dollar per unit technique assumes that the units in the subject and comparables have the same income potential. However, a building with 10 one-bedroom units will sell for less than a building with 10 two-bedroom units (all else being equal), and making a direct comparison between the two with this indicator is invalid. The problem becomes more serious when one realizes that the subject and comparables will hardly if ever have identical unit mixes. A way of circumventing this problem is to adjust the indicator according to the ratio of dollar earnings per unit. The following is an example of adjusting the dollar per unit indicator when the comparable and subject have different unit mixes and rental rates.

Example 4-10. *Adjusting the dollar per unit indicator.*

A comparable is found that sold for $37,500 per unit. The subject property and comparable have the following unit mixes:

	Subject			**Comparable**		
	Number of Units	Unit Rent	Total Rent	Number of Units	Unit Rent	Total Rent
One bedroom	4	$360	$1,440	9	$330	$2,970
Two bedrooms	6	440	2,640	5	440	2,200
Three bedrooms	0	0	0	1	500	500
Totals	10		$4,080	15		$5,670
Average rent per unit			$408			$378

Q.   What is the adjusted number of dollars paid per unit for the comparable sale?

A.   First, find the income ratio of the subject rent per unit to that of the comparable:

$$\frac{\text{Subject average rent per unit}}{\text{Comparable average rent per unit}} = \frac{408}{378} = 1.08$$

Second, The adjusted dollars per unit is found by multiplying the comparable's dollar sale price per unit by the above factor:

$$\$37,500 \times 1.08 = \$40,500$$

The subject number of units times this amount results in a subject property value indication of $405,000 ($40,500 per unit × 10 units).

   A similar adjustment can be made with the dollars per room or dollars per square foot indicators with the adjustment ratio merely computed on the average rent per room or rent per square foot.

Adjusting for Financing

Financing is critical in the estimate of value. It has been said that any price will be paid if the financing is right. When properties generally were sold with conventional, standard-rate mortgages and little creative secondary financing, there was not as much need for adjusting comparable sales for financing—their financing was not appreciably different from the subject's. This scenario has changed, and it is a matter of equalizing the effects of different types of financing before fair comparisons of comparables and subject can be made.

The method used for making this adjustment is called cash equivalency. Because of the complexities of this technique and the possible need for a financial calculator, cash equivalence is discussed in Chapter 16. The importance of this procedure should be immediately obvious, however, and it is one more reason for taking the minutes required to learn the keys of the financial calculator.

VALUATION SUBJECT TO EXISTING FINANCING

To this point, the determination of multipliers and overall rates has been directed largely toward properties that are to receive new financing upon purchase. Under this assumption, most apartment buildings in a particular market share common expectations about financing and cash flows, and the market-derived multipliers, overall rates, and physical approaches to value can be fairly reliable. However, these approaches may need some alteration if the property is to be valued subject to its existing loan. When the property is valued in this way, the estimate is often expressed as the sum of the loan amount plus equity value:

$$\text{Total value} = \text{loan amount} + \text{equity value}$$

Since the balance of the existing loan will be known, the real task is to determine the value of the equity. This is usually done by the present value method (Chapter 11) or through the use of an appropriate cash-flow rate.

On the surface it may appear logical to use the same cash-flow rate for valuing a property selling subject to the existing loan that would be used in the same market to value a property selling subject to a new loan. However, there are several underlying factors that invalidate this practice. Consider the case of an apartment building with a $90,000 annual net income. Using the band of investment technique, the overall rate based on a a new, 12% interest, 30-year loan for 75% of value (constant of 0.1234) and a 5% cash-flow rate would be 10.51%:

$$
\begin{aligned}
0.75 \times 0.1234 &= 0.0926 \\
0.25 \times 0.500 &= \underline{0.0125} \\
\text{OAR} &= 0.1051
\end{aligned}
$$

This would provide a value estimate of approximately $850,000.

Assume the same property has an existing loan of $410,000 with annual payments of $50,630. A 5% cash-flow rate requirement will provide an equity value of $787,400 and a total property value of approximately $1,200,000:

Net income	$90,000
Annual loan payments	(50,630)
Cash flow	$39,370

$$\text{Equity value} = \frac{\$39,370}{0.05} = \$787,400$$

Loan amount	$ 410,000
Equity value	787,400
Value estimate	$1,197,400
Round to	$1,200,000

Although both purchases would provide the investor with a 5% first year return on equity (cash-flow rate), other factors involved would have an impact on the investor's true return and hence on value. These can be summarized as follows:

1. The basis for depreciation increases with purchase price.
2. Appreciation benefits are diluted as the percentage of equity investment to purchase price increases.
3. Benefits from cash-flow growth are diluted as the percentage of equity investment to purchase price increases.
4. Takeover of the existing loan generally requires no qualification or loan fees on the part of the purchaser.
5. Property marketability (sale or exchange) is increased through a high loan-to-value ratio.
6. Interest payments provide additional tax shelter.

These factors tend to make the selection of an appropriate cash-flow rate somewhat difficult, adding favor to the present value technique, which measures the value of a series of annual after-tax cash flows. On the contrary, however, some markets are composed of investors who make purchases based largely on a certain cash-flow rate regardless of the loan-to-value ratio, serving to reinstate the validity of using the cash-flow rate to estimate market value. Again, the selection of valuation methods and their rates and factors rests heavily on judgment and market investigation.

DEBT COVERAGE RATIO

The debt coverage ratio (DCR) is an analysis tool and, similar to the band of investment technique, can also be used to build an overall rate.

The debt coverage ratio is the number that results from dividing the NOI by the annual loan payments. For example, consider an investment with a $50,000 NOI and $40,000 of annual loan payments:

$$\text{DCR} = \frac{\text{NOI}}{\text{loan payments}} = \frac{\$50,000}{\$40,000} = 1.25$$

The DCR tells us that the NOI is 1.25 times the annual loan payments. There are several ways in which the debt coverage ratio can be used:

Analyzing the cash flow
Determining the maximum loan amount
Building an overall rate

1. Analyzing the Cash Flow. Both lenders and investors use the DCR. A lender typically may underwrite the financing based on a DCR of between 1.00 and 1.25 to ensure that the property will provide at least enough cash flow to cover the loan payments. A DCR of 1.00 is obviously a break-even cash flow; a DCR of less than 1.00 means that the annual NOI is insufficient to cover the loan payments, and a DCR over 1.00 provides a safety cushion for the lender and investor.

Because of the importance of financing, it is advisable for brokers and investors to be acquainted with the lender's DCR requirements. This may help save time in finding an investment that provides maximum leverage. Note that the actual maximum loan to be made available by the lender may differ from that anticipated by the broker or investor due to variations in the respective NOI estimates.

The investor may use the DCR to analyze the cash flow in the same way that the cash-flow rate is used. Also, when making annual cash-flow projections, some analysts find it desirable to include the DCR for each year.

2. Determining the Maximum Loan Amount. Many lenders will provide financing based on a minimum debt coverage ratio requirement. The lender figures the maximum loan amount based on net income, the annual loan constant, and the DCR requirement:

$$\text{Maximum loan amount} = \frac{\text{NOI}}{\text{annual constant} \times \text{DCR}}$$

Example 4-11. *Finding the maximum available loan based on a DCR requirement.*

The lender is willing to make a 12.5%, 30-year loan (annual constant of 0.1281). The lender, for security reasons, wants the property to produce an NOI of at least 1.15 times the loan payments. The annual NOI is $85,400.

Q. What is the maximum loan the lender will make based on the 1.15 DCR requirement?

A. $\dfrac{\$85,400}{0.1281 \times 1.15} = \$579,710$

The indicated loan will probably be rounded down to $579,000 or even $575,000.

3. Building an Overall Rate.

In this technique, an overall rate is built up based on the available loan terms (annual constant and maximum loan-to-value ratio) and the minimum DCR requirement:

OAR = annual constant × maximum loan-to-value ratio × DCR

The following example demonstrates the building of an overall rate:

Example 4-12. *Deriving an OAR and value estimate with the DCR.*

The lender is willing to make a 12.5%, 30-year loan (annual constant of 0.1281) for 80% of the appraised value and wants the property to provide a DCR of 1.15 for security reasons. The annual NOI is $85,400. Based on the lender's DCR requirement

Q. What is the overall rate?

A. OAR = 0.1281 × 0.80 × 1.15 = 0.1179

Q. What is the value estimate?

A. Value estimate $= \dfrac{\text{NOI}}{\text{OAR}} = \dfrac{\$85,400}{0.1179} = 725,000$ (rounded)

The similarity between this technique and the band of investment technique for building an overall rate should be readily apparent. In both cases the annual constant is weighted by the loan-to-value ratio to find what percentage of the purchase price or value must be paid annually to service the loan, with any additional points above a 1.00 DCR reflecting the return on the equity investment (cash flow).

LAND VALUATION

In the case of new construction it is necessary to estimate a value or maximum purchase price for the land. This is often done with comparable land sales that are broken down into value indicators such as dollars per square foot or dollars per unit (municipalities generally have density limits allowing a maximum number of units per thousand square feet, acre, etc.).

In addition to the market techniques for land valuation, the *land residual technique* may be used and is recommended even if a market valuation has been made of the land as it further offers an appropriate analysis of the proposed project.

In this technique, the net income is estimated for the completed property as proposed and is then capitalized into an estimate of value using an overall rate. This OAR may be a market-derived rate (especially if the property is to be sold upon completion) or produced through the band of investment (more applicable to the investor who wishes to retain the property and requires a certain return). The estimated cost to complete the proposed improvements,* including developer's profit, is deducted from the total value with the residual value attributed to the land:

Example 4-13. *Valuing land using the land residual technique.*
A well-located vacant parcel is found on which a maximum of 35 units can be built. Based on the formulation of an income and expense statement, the first year's net income for the property is estimated to be $85,000. Construction cost for the building and site improvements is $710,000, and the developer requires a profit of 15% of the total completed value. The OAR expected for such a project is 9.0%.

Q. Using the land residual technique, determine the maximum amount that can be paid for the land?

---

*Cost estimates for apartment buildings can be obtained through a continually updated cost service. The one most universally used is the *Residential Cost Handbook* published by Marshall and Swift Publication Company, 1617 Beverly Boulevard, Los Angeles 90026

A. Total value $= \dfrac{\text{NOI}}{\text{OAR}} = \dfrac{\$85{,}000}{0.0900} = \$944{,}000$ (r)

(Land value + building cost) (1 + developer's profit) = total value

(Land value + $710,000) (1.15) = $944,000

Land value + $710,000 $= \dfrac{\$944{,}000}{1.15}$

Land value $= \$111{,}000$ (r)

PART TWO

INVESTMENT ANALYSIS

CHAPTER FIVE

INTRODUCTION TO INVESTMENT ANALYSIS

The most commonly recognized method and the one used by top real estate professionals for analyzing the performance and alternatives of income-producing properties involves making projections and assumptions about the acquisition terms and future of the property:

At what rate will the income and expenses grow?
What type of depreciation will be used?
How will the property be financed?
What is the investor's tax bracket?

The annual after-tax cash flows (ATCFs) can then be estimated for the projected holding period and the final measure of investment performance, the rate of return, can then be calculated. This analysis method is commonly called discounted cash flow (DCF).

A step-by step pictorial version of the DCF process is presented in the figures in this chapter and is depictive of the construction of the annual after-tax cash flows and the rate of return calculation for Case Study 1. The chapters that follow use the same case study and dollar amounts in demonstrating the mechanics for constructing the ATCF and the rate of return computation as well as show how the investment provides tax shelter and income over the holding period. First, the projections and assumptions used in the investment are summarized:

Assumptions and Projections for Case Study 1

PROPERTY	12 units, 15 years old, side walk-up in average area.
PURCHASE PRICE	$300,000
CASH DOWN	$90,000 plus $3,000 closing costs incidental to the sale
LOAN	$210,000 first mortgage at 11.75%, 30-year amortization, monthly payments. Annual payment is $25,437.
INCOME	$36,691 effective gross income (at purchase) increasing at 8.5% per year with the first increase effective at the end of year 1.
EXPENSES	$11,731 per year (at purchase) increasing 12% per year. First increase effect at the end of year 1.
DEPRECIATION	Use ACRS 15-year depreciation schedule. Improvements represent 60% of the total value.
RESALE	Investment to sell at the same overall rate as purchased at (8.32%). Sale costs are 7%.
TAX RATE	Investor has a 50% marginal tax rate.
STRATEGY	Maintain property in present condition and sell at the end of five years.
RATE OF RETURN	Financial management rate of return. Cash-flow reinvestment rate is 8% per annum.

Effective gross income (Figure 5-1) is assumed to escalate at the rate of 8.5% per year over the five-year holding period. A 2% per year allowance for vacancy and collection loss is included.

Net operating income is the effective gross income less operating expenses. Whereas the effective gross income is assumed to be increasing at the rate of 8.5% per year, the operating expenses are assumed to escalate at the annual rate of 12%, or 3.5% faster than the income itself. However, note that since operating expenses represent only a portion of the effective gross income, the net operating income still increases from year to year (see Figure 5-2).

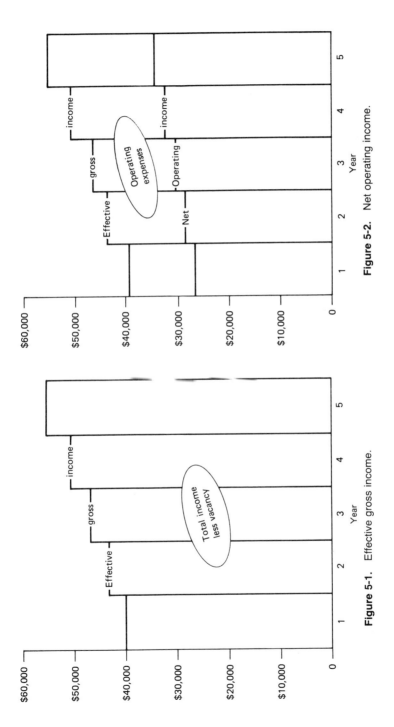

Figure 5-1. Effective gross income.

Figure 5-2. Net operating income.

Net operating income (NOI) is the income provided by the operation of the property but does not take into account any loan payments resulting from the financing of the investment. Deducting loan payments from NOI results in the before-tax cash flow (BTCF). Since the loan payments are constant from year to year (assuming a conventional loan), the BTCF increases by the same dollar amount as the NOI (see Figure 5-3).

Not yet included are the all-important income tax consequences. In Figure 5-4 we will deduct any interest payments and depreciation allowance from the NOI to arrive at the taxable income. Taxable income is the amount of income generated by the property reported to the IRS.

Note that the property is considered to be operating at a loss for all five years. This loss is deducted from the investor's other ordinary income thus providing the investor with a tax shelter. The tax savings (amount of tax payment avoided as a result of the investment) provided by the operating loss is determined by multiplying the annual loss by the investor's marginal tax rate. This amount can be considered a cash flow attributable to the property.

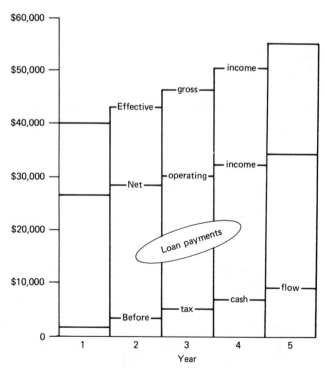

Figure 5-3.   Before-tax cash flow.

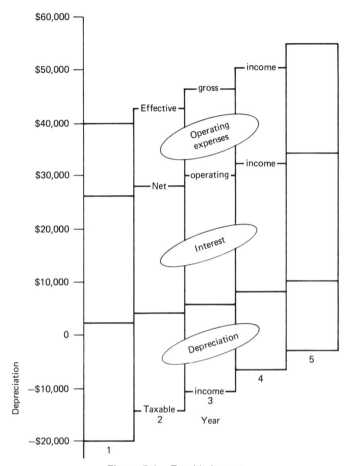

Figure 5-4. Taxable income.

If the taxable income had been a positive amount in any year, the IRS would have considered the property to be operating at a profit. Again, the investor's marginal tax rate would be applied to the taxable income, but this time to find the amount of tax payable as a result of the investment. The tax would be deducted from the before-tax cash flow to arrive at the after-tax cash flow, and there would be no tax shelter provided by the investment.

Note that without the tax shelter there would be no negative taxable income, which means that none of the investor's other ordinary income would be sheltered at any time during the holding period.

Using the marginal tax rate to find the tax savings or tax payable, we can now go on to compute the after-tax cash flow in Figure 5-5.

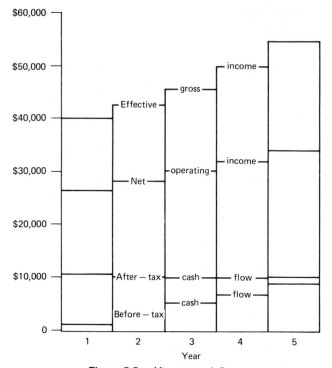

Figure 5-5. After-tax cash flow.

The final step in deriving the after-tax cash flow is to add any tax savings to or deduct any tax payable from the before-tax cash flow.

The taxable income in Figure 5-4 for all five years is negative. This means that other income is sheltered, and there is a tax savings provided by the investment. This tax savings is *added* to the respective before-tax cash flows in arriving at the after-tax cash flow.

A positive taxable income figure for any year would have resulted in a tax payable for that year rather than a tax savings, and this amount would be *deducted* from the before-tax cash flow in computing the after-tax cash flow.

Now that the after-tax cash flows have been determined, it is necessary to apply some measurement of performance to them. The measurement demonstrated here is the financial management rate of return (FMRR). The first step in applying this rate of return to the cash flows is to assume that *each cash flow is reinvested for the duration of the investment holding period* at a plausible reinvestment rate. Here it is assumed to be 8.5%.

At the end of the holding period, the *reinvested after-tax cash flows,* the

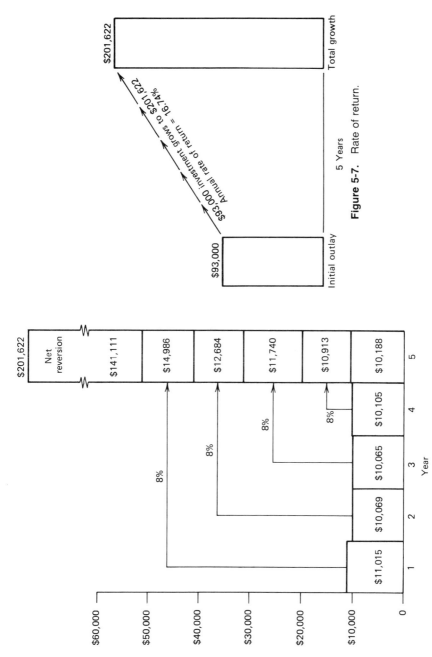

Figure 5-7. Rate of return.

Figure 5-6. Annual after-tax cash flows reinvested at 8% per annum.

final year's after-tax cash flow (assumed to be realized at the end of the last year) and the *net reversion* realized upon resale total $201,622 (Figure 5-6).

At resale, it is time for the investor to get back not only the original investment of $93,000 but the return on that investment as well.

We can see that the initial investment of $93,000 has grown to a total sum worth $201,622. The rate of return is the rate at which the $93,000 compounded annually for five years grows to equal the sum of $201,622. That rate is 16.74% (Figure 5-7).

Proof

End of Year	Growth
Start	$ 93,000
1	+ 16.74%
	108,566
2	+ 16.74%
	126,737
3	+ 16.74%
	147,950
4	+ 16.74%
	172,714
5	+ 16.74%
	$201,622

CHAPTER SIX

INTEREST

LOAN PAYMENTS

Loan payments are composed of:

1. A payment to reduce (amortize) the loan principal.
2. A payment of interest on the remaining balance of the loan.

In typical real estate loans the principal payment is initially a very small part of the payment (representing only 3% of the first year's payments in Case Study 1) with the interest portion being the decisively major portion of the payment. As the loan balance decreases over a period of time, so does the amount of interest payment as it is calculated on the remaining balance. Since the loan payments are a constant or level amount (with the exception being certain variable rate or term financing techniques), the principal payments (amortization) increase over the life of the loan (Figure 6-2).

LOAN BALANCE CALCULATION

The reasons for wanting to determine the loan balance are twofold:

1. A by-product of the balance calculation is the amount of interest paid. We are concerned with this amount because it is a deductible expense in the operation of an income property and is vital in the construction of the after-tax cash flow.

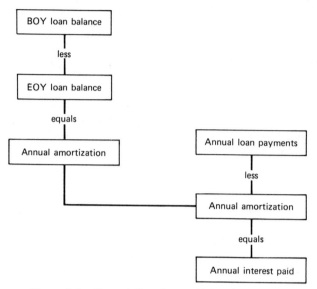

Figure 6-1. Computation of annual interest payments.

2. The loan balance upon resale of the property must be deducted from the sale price in figuring the net reversion (sale proceeds) to the seller.

   Loan balance calculations can be done quickly with a financial calculator and is covered in Calculator Procedure 2 in the Appendix. Some loan payment books include balance tables. Still another method (using the payment tables themselves) is included at the end of this chapter. It is necessary to use one of these techniques to figure the end-of-year loan balance for each year of the holding period before proceeding to the interest calculation.

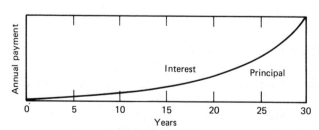

Figure 6-2. Principal/interest portions of loan payments.

INTEREST CALCULATION

The amount of interest paid on the loan is computed as the amount of annual loan payments less the amount of amortization for that year. In other words, the portion of the annual payments that does not reduce the principal is interest.

This process is depicted in Figure 6-1. The process must be performed for each year of the projected holding period to arrive at the respective annual cash flows. Remember, with no time gap between consecutive years, the BOY balance is the same as the EOY balance for the previous year. Step-by-step, the process is:

1. Compute the BOY loan balance.
2. Compute the EOY loan balance and subtract this amount from the BOY balance. Result: amount of annual amortization.
3. Find the annual total of the loan payments and subtract the amount of annual amortization. Result: interest paid in that year.
4. Repeat the above steps for each year in the holding period using the EOY balance figure from the previous year as the BOY figure for the next year. The process must be repeated for any secondary mortgages.

Certain financial calculators have the capacity for more expeditious balance and interest computations than have been demonstrated here. These techniques should be covered in the calculator's instruction book.

Example 6-1, Case Study 1.   *Finding the amount of interest paid in successive years.*

A loan is obtained for $210,000 at 11.75% interest to be amortized over 30 years. Annual payments are $25,437.

Q.   What are the interest payments for the first three years?

A.   Loan balance calculations are computed using Calculator Procedure 2:

Year 1 amortization		*Year 1 interest*	
BOY 1 loan balance	$210,000	Annual loan payments	$25,437
EOY 1 loan balance	(209,196)	Year 1 amortization	(804)
Year 1 amortization	$ 804	Year 1 interest paid	$24,633

Year 2 amortization

BOY 2 loan balance	$209,196
EOY 2 loan balance	(208,292)
Year 2 amortization	$ 903

Year 2 interest

Annual loan payments	$25,437
Year 2 amortization	(903)
Year 2 interest paid	$24,534

Year 3 amortization

BOY 3 loan balance	$208,292
EOY 3 loan balance	(207,276)
Year 3 amortization	$ 1,016

Year 3 interest

Annual loan payments	$25,437
Year 2 amortization	(1,016)
Year 3 interest paid	$24,421

The Year 1 amortization figure is inserted into the interest calculation for the particular year. The resulting interest and amortization schedule is as follows.

Interest and Amortization Schedule

Year	EOY Loan Balance	Amortization	Interest
(Start)	$210,000		
1	209,196	$ 804	$24,633
2	208,292	903	24,534
3	207,276	1,016	24,421

Note that each year's amortization plus interest total the annual loan payment of $25,437.

MONTHLY AMORTIZING PAYMENTS 11.75%

AMOUNT OF LOAN	NUMBER OF YEARS IN TERM						
	20	25	28	29	30	35	40
$ 25	.28	.26	.26	.26	.26	.25	.25
50	.55	.52	.51	.51	.51	.50	.50
75	.82	.78	.77	.76	.76	.75	.75
			1.04	1.02	1.01	.99	.99
			2.07	2.04	2.03		.98
60000	650.23					597.46	
65000	704.41	672.			656.12	647.27	642.
70000	758.60	724.3b		69.31	706.59	697.06	691.8b
75000	812.79	776.10	763.27	759.97	757.06	746.85	741.28
80000	866.97	827.84	814.16	810.64	807.53	796.64	790.70
85000	921.16	879.58	865.04	861.30	858.00	846.43	840.11
90000	975.34	931.32	915.93	911.97	908.47	896.22	889.53
95000	1029.53	983.06	966.81	962.63	958.94	946.01	938.95
100000	1083.71	1034.80	1017.70	1013.30	1009.41	995.80	988.37

Figure 6-3. Loan payment book.

LOAN BALANCE CALCULATIONS FROM A PAYMENT BOOK

If you are caught without a financial calculator or set of loan balance tables, the next way to figure loan balances is by using the loan payment book (Figure 6-3). Divide the payment for the total term of the loan by the payment required if the term were the number of years remaining after the date of the desired balance calculation. Use the figures for the largest principal amount given, which will result in the greatest accuracy. This computation gives the percentage of the loan balance remaining. Multiply the original loan amount by this percentage. Result: the remaining loan balance.

$$\frac{1009.41}{1017.70} = 0.9918542$$

Remaining balance $= 0.9918542 \times \$210{,}000 = \$208{,}289$

Note that the calculator answer is $208,291.

CHAPTER SEVEN

DEPRECIATION

Depreciation allowance is the investor's favorite form of tax shelter because it is treated like a cash outflow similar to expenses for IRS purposes, although it involves no actual cash outlay. Depreciation permits accounting losses on the real estate investment that can be offset against income generated from other sources and may defer taxable earnings from yearly ordinary income to capital gains.

Depreciation procedures were radically changed in 1981 with the enactment of the Economic Recovery Tax Act. Apartment buildings and personal property (furniture, stoves, refrigerators, etc.) are now depreciated under the Accelerated Cost Recovery System (ACRS). Under this system, apartment buildings are accorded a 15-year life and are subject to the depreciation schedule presented in Exhibit 7-1.

DEPRECIABLE BASIS

The basis of a property purchased outright is its cost (without regard to financing), although property acquired through gifts, exchanges, inheritance, or other methods involves other considerations when computing the basis. As the land portion of the investment is not depreciable, the investment cost must be apportioned between land and improvements. Apportionment methods include:

1. Use of assessor's ratios if within reason. This method is most often used by the IRS.

Exhibit 7-1. ACRS 15-Year Real Property Depreciation Factors for All Real Estate (Except Low-Income Housing)*

If the Recovery Year Is	The Applicable Percentage Is											
	Month 1	Month 2	Month 3	Month 4	Month 5	Month 6	Month 7	Month 8	Month 9	Month 10	Month 11	Month 12
1	12	11	10	9	8	7	6	5	4	3	2	1
2	10	10	11	11	11	11	11	11	11	11	11	12
3	9	9	9	9	10	10	10	10	10	10	10	10
4	8	8	8	8	8	8	9	9	9	9	9	9
5	7	7	7	7	7	7	8	8	8	8	8	8
6	6	6	6	6	7	7	7	7	7	7	7	7
7	6	6	6	6	6	6	6	6	6	6	6	6
8	6	6	6	6	6	6	5	6	6	6	6	6
9	6	6	6	6	5	5	5	5	5	6	6	6
10	5	6	5	5	5	5	5	5	5	5	5	5
11	5	5	5	5	5	5	5	5	5	5	5	5
12	5	5	5	5	5	5	5	5	5	5	5	5
13	5	5	5	5	5	5	5	5	5	5	5	5
14	5	5	5	5	5	5	5	5	5	5	5	5
15	5	5	5	5	5	5	5	5	5	5	5	5
16	—	—	1	1	2	2	3	3	4	4	4	5

*Low-income housing is subject to a different depreciation schedule, which is not included here.

2. An appraisal by a qualified appraiser.
3. Contractual agreement between buyer and seller (must be considered to affect both parties).

Actually, the basis not only includes the purchase price but also items incidental to obtaining title such as escrow and legal fees, recording fees, purchase commissions, title insurance, and survey and appraisal fees. The IRS has contended that, after apportionment of land and improvements, these costs should be added to the land portion of the basis and not depreciated.

COMPUTING DEPRECIATION

Depreciation computations are easily handled by multiplying the depreciable basis against the depreciation factor (Exhibit 7-1) for the particular year. For cash flow projections, it is fair and consistent to base the depreciation allowance on the January factors. The following is an example using Case Study 1.

Example 7-1. *Computing the annual depreciation allowance.*
A purchaser buys an apartment building with a $195,000 depreciable basis.

Q. What is the annual depreciation allowance for the first five years? Use the January factors.

A.	Year	Depreciable Basis	Depreciation Factor	Annual Depreciation
	1	$180,000	12%	$21,600
	2	180,000	10	18,000
	3	180,000	9	16,200
	4	180,000	8	14,400
	5	180,000	7	12,600

OPTIONAL STRAIGHT-LINE DEPRECIATION

Although straight-line depreciation will reduce the depreciation allowance effectively over the critical first few years, the taxpayer may elect to use this method of depreciation in combination with either a 15-, 35- or 45-year recovery period.

If straight-line depreciation is elected, the annual depreciation allowance is computed by dividing 1 by the recovery period (resulting in $\frac{1}{15}$, $\frac{1}{35}$, or $\frac{1}{45}$) and multiplying this result by the depreciable basis. Hence the allowance will be a constant amount from year to year.

CHANGES TO THE BASIS

During the holding period the basis will change due to deductions and additions.

Capital improvements increase the basis by their cost.
Depreciation reduces the basis by the amount written off.

The net result of these changes is called the adjusted basis and is of importance in the year-to-year depreciation computation as well as in calculating the gain or loss for tax purposes upon disposition of the property.

CAPITALIZING OR EXPENSING

To adjust the taxable basis properly it is necessary to make distinctions between expenditures that are either added to the basis (capital improvements) or deducted from the gross income in the year incurred (expenses). Money spent on the property will be considered either a capital improvement or an expense. The investor will usually prefer to take any expenditure as a current expense to cause an immediate reduction in tax liability. The alternative, capitalizing an expenditure (adding it to the adjusted basis), not only defers any write-off advantage but also dilutes it due to the reduced rate at which capital gains are taxed.

Items that can be currently expensed (deducted from income in the year incurred) are repair and maintenance work that do little or nothing to add to the remaining life of the property and only serve to maintain its value and keep it in ordinary operating condition.

Capital improvements (additions to the basis) are items that upgrade the property or add to its remaining useful life. Note that repairs may be considered capital improvements if they are part of a general plan to improve or rehabilitate the property.

PERSONAL PROPERTY DEPRECIATION

Personal property is anything that is not real property and is often characterized by its mobility or lack of permanent attachment to the real property. Stoves, refrigerators, and furniture are examples of personal property found in apartment buildings.

Personal property depreciation was also affected by the Economic Recovery Tax Act of 1981 and is similar to real property depreciation with several exceptions.

The Internal Revenue Code does not stipulate specific recovery periods for various kinds of apartment building personal property but lumps it into a broad category including other kinds of personal property (even trucks) as well. This category is labeled "Section 1245 Property" (real estate is Section 1250 Property). Section 1245 property is depreciated over a period of 3, 5, or 10 years. What is the proper recovery period for items like furniture, stoves, and refrigerators? Some tax preparers had used three years successfully on these items even before the 1981 rules (when the rules were equally nonexplicit), although the IRS seems to be leaning progressively more toward a five-year recovery period for personal property. The used personal property acquired with the building in Case Studies 3 and 4 are given a three-year recovery period for convenience in analysis, although this might not stand in court. The new personal property acquired during renovation will be depreciated over a five-year recovery period.

Note that the 20% additional first year write-off for personal property was dropped upon the enactment of the Economic Recovery Tax Act of 1981.

Exhibits 7-2, 7-3, and 7-4 are a summary of 3-, 5-, and 10-year depreciation factors for personal property.

LOAN POINTS AND FEES

When financing for the property is provided by an institutional lender, there is often a charge for points and/or fees at the time of loan funding. Neither of these costs has been assumed in the case studies, but these items, especially points, are usually of a significant amount.

Points

Each loan point is an up-front charge representing 1% of the loan amount and most often is considered to be prepaid interest, although in some localities and situations a point may be considered wholly or partially a loan

Exhibit 7-2.   Personal Property Placed in Service 1981–1984

	The Depreciation Factor Is		
If the Recovery Year Is	3-Year	5-Year	10-Year
1	25	15	8
2	38	22	14
3	37	21	12
4		21	10
5		21	10
6			10
7			9
8			9
9			9
10			9

fee (loan origination or placement fee). The lender involved can tell you specifically what the points represent. When considered a loan origination or placement fee, points are deductible in full as an expense in the year incurred. When considered prepaid interest, the points must be expensed over the life of the loan. Had a charge of 1½ points been made for the loan in Case Study 1, the charge would have been allocated over the holding period in the following way.

Exhibit 7-3.   Personal Property Placed in Service 1985

	The Depreciation Factor Is		
If the Recovery Year Is	3-Year	5-Year	10-Year
1	29	18	9
2	47	33	19
3	24	25	16
4		16	14
5		8	12
6			10
7			8
8			6
9			4
10			2

Exhibit 7-4.   Personal Property Placed in Service after 1985

If the Recovery Year Is	The Depreciation Factor Is		
	3-Year	5-Year	10-Year
1	33	20	10
2	45	32	18
3	22	24	16
4		16	14
5		8	12
6			10
7			8
8			6
9			4
10			2

Example 7-2. *Treatment of loan points in the cash flow.*

Assume 1½ points have been charged on a 30-year, $210,000 loan (this computes to point charge of $3,150). The projected holding period is five years. The points are considered to be prepaid interest.

Q. What is the annual write-off?

A. Annual write-off $= \dfrac{\$3,150}{30 \text{ years}} = \$105$

Q. What is the unamortized portion at resale and how is it treated?

A. Amount not amortized: $3,150 − (5 × $105) = $2,625
The $2,625 is added to the adjusted basis when computing the capital gain.

Treatment of Points as Loan Fees

When points are considered loan fees, they are added to the nondepreciable portion of the basis as purchasing costs incidental to the transaction. As a result, no write-off is taken on loan fees until disposition, at which time the effect will be a reduction in capital gain due to the increased basis.

CHAPTER EIGHT

AFTER-TAX CASH FLOW

When the net income projection, interest paid, and depreciation have been determined, there are but a few more computations needed to arrive at the after-tax cash flow (ATCF). It is now a matter of fitting together the pieces.

Taxable income from the investment is not the same as the after-tax cash flow to the investor. Taxable income refers to reportable income—income generated by the property that is reported to the IRS. In fact, the most advantageous situation, and the produced by many apartment investments, is having negative taxable income but actually receiving a positive after-tax cash flow. This negative/positive difference is possible because of the depreciation deduction that decreases the reportable income, an advantage that carries over to the actual after-tax income.

DETERMINING ANNUAL TAXABLE INCOME

Determining the annual taxable income generated by the property is done here solely for the purpose of computing either the amount of tax payable or tax savings provided to the investor as a result of the investment. Taxable income is the net operating income less interest payments and depreciation allowances. Note that taxable income will be either a positive or negative amount. Examine the Case Study 1 taxable income in Year 1 and Year 5:

	Year 1	Year 5
Net operating income	$26,671	$34,496
Mortgage interest	(24,633)	(24,153)
Depreciation	(21,600)	(12,600)
Taxable income	($19,562)	($ 2,257)

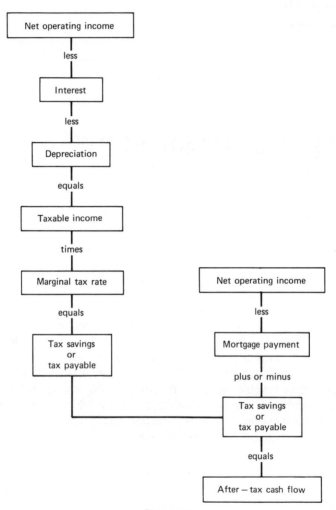

Figure 8-1

A negative taxable income results when the net income is less than the deductions for depreciation and interest. The IRS considers the property to be operating at a loss, and such a loss is deductible from the investor's other ordinary income. Not only does the investor avoid paying any income tax on the property but on a sheltered portion of other ordinary income as well.

A positive taxable income (not displayed but which would occur in later years) results when the net income is greater than the deductions for depreciation and interest. The IRS now considers the property to be operating at a profit and demands that the investor add this profit to other income.

USING THE MARGINAL TAX RATE TO FIND THE NET EFFECT OF TAXABLE INCOME

The investor's net effect of the taxable income, be it negative or positive, can be calculated by multiplying the taxable income by the investor's marginal tax rate. The marginal tax rate is the percentage of income paid in taxes on the investor's uppermost bracket of income. The upper bracket is used because the investment most often is considered to represent additional income. The marginal tax rate can be determined by reference to the appropriate tax rate schedule for the investor.

Example 8-1, Case Study 1. *Determining tax savings or tax payable.*
Cashflow projections provide the following estimates of annual taxable income.

	Year 1	Year 5
Net operating income	$26,671	$34,496
Mortgage interest	(24,633)	(24,153)
Depreciation	(21,600)	(12,600)
Taxable income	($19,562)	($ 2,257)

Q. Using a marginal tax rate of 50%, what are the tax savings or tax payable provided to the investor by these estimates?

A. The tax savings are calculated:

	Year 1	Year 5
Taxable income	($19,562)	($ 2,257)
Marginal tax rate	× 50%	× 50%
Tax savings	$ 9,781	$ 1,129
Tax payable	—	—

Multiplying a negative taxable income by the marginal tax rate shows a tax savings—the amount that the investor saves from having to pay the IRS in a given year. Had there been a positive taxable income in one of the years, this amount would also be multiplied by the marginal tax rate but would result in the amount of taxes *paid* on the taxable income generated by the investment.

The amount of tax savings or tax payable is the net effect of the property's IRS tax consequence and is carried forward to the after-tax cash flow computation.

CONSTRUCTING THE AFTER-TAX CASH FLOW (ATCF)

The ATCF is the result of the before-tax cash flow (net income less loan payments) with the inclusion of the tax effect outlined in the last few examples. Whereas a tax savings would be *added* to the before-tax cash flow, a tax payable figure would be *deducted* from the before-tax cash flow. The ATCF calculation is as follows.

	Year 1	Year 5
Net income	$26,671	$34,496
Loan payments	(25,437)	(25,437)
Before-tax cash flow	$ 1,234	$ 9,059
Tax savings	9,781	1,129
Tax payable	—	—
After-tax cash flow	$11,015	$10,188

CHAPTER NINE

REVERSION

The investor will sell the property but won't pocket the whole proceeds. What one actually receives after transaction costs, loan payoffs, and taxes is called the net reversion.

PROJECTING SALE PRICE

The final sale price can be projected the way the analyst sees fit but most probably will be determined by applying an overall rate to the final year's (or year following the final year) net income (discussed in Chapter 4). This overall rate could be the same as that abstracted from the initial purchase price or could be higher or lower depending on the projected market conditions and changes in the property. The forecast mortgage market and the financing on the property at time of resale can influence the reversion estimate. For Case Study 1 we use the same OAR produced by the initial purchase:

Example 9-1, Case Study 1. *Determining the OAR and projecting sale price*
A property is purchased for $300,000 and shows a first year net income of $24,960.

Q. What is the overall rate indicated by the initial purchase?

A. $\text{OAR} = \dfrac{\text{NOI}}{\text{sale price}} = \dfrac{\$24,960}{\$300,000} = 0.0832$

Q. Based on the indicated OAR and a Year 5 net income of $34,497, what is the projected sale price?

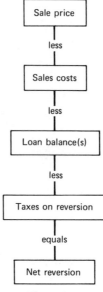

Figure 9-1

A. Projected sale price $= \dfrac{\text{NOI}}{\text{OAR}} = \dfrac{\$34,497}{0.0832} = \$414,627$. Round to $415,000.

Caution: The use of an abstracted gross rent multiplier loses validity for the projection if income and expenses are assumed to fluctuate at different rates.

SALE COSTS

Sale costs are those costs incidental to the sale such as commissions and legal and title fees. These are deducted from the sale price, thereby reducing the gain. They are not to be added to the final year's expenses (except for dealers). Only prorated operating expenses such as for property taxes, insurance, and utilities are considered expenses that are deducted from the final year's income rather than added as a sale cost. The sale price less sale costs equals the net sale price. For Case Study 1, assume that sale costs total 7% of the $415,000 projected sale price:

Sale price	$415,000
Sale cost %	× 7%
Sale cost	$ 29,050

This amount is deducted from the sale price to determine the net sale price:

Sale price	$415,000
Sale cost	(29,050)
Net sale price	$385,950

LOAN BALANCE

The loan balance is figured using Calculator Procedure 2 or is carried forward from the annual interest calculations where it plays a vital role. For Case Study 1, the remaining loan balance is $204,849.

TAXES ON REVERSION

Actual tax calculation involving gains or losses could be moderately complicated due to the netting of short- and long-term gains and losses, the alternative minimum tax (rarely applicable to salaried taxpayers), and other factors. However, the analysis process involves projections into the future, and it is difficult to predict gains, losses, and other tax consequences in the year of projected resale. To simplify the process and to avoid compounding any projection error, the analyst generally chooses to treat the subject transaction as its own net figure, thereby excluding any external factors resulting from other influences in the investor's remaining portfolio.

Capital Gains Tax

There are different types of capital gains transactions—short- and long-term losses and short- and long-term gains. Real estate almost always results in a gain (net sale price being greater than the adjusted basis), and the investor usually holds on to the property for more than 12 months to achieve the preferential treatment of long-term status. Therefore, the capital transaction discussion is restricted to long-term gains only.

How the Capital Gains Tax Works

First, there is no capital gains tax. The long-term capital gain benefit is that only 40% of the gain is reportable and is then taxed at the ordinary rate. For each gain of $1,000, only $400 need be reported for tax purposes.

When Section 1231 property (which includes income-producing real estate) is disposed of, the gain or loss is figured as the difference between the net sale price and the adjusted basis at time of disposition. And, if the Accelerated Cost Recovery System (ACRS) method of depreciation has been used (as opposed to the straight-line method), the amount of recaptured excess depreciation is first deducted from the gain so that it can be taxed separately, in full, at the ordinary rate. To compute the taxable gain, it is first necessary to determine the amount of recaptured excess depreciation.

DEPRECIATION RECAPTURE

For apartment buildings, gain on disposition is ordinary income to the extent that depreciation taken with the ACRS schedule exceeds the depreciation that would have been allowed had the straight-line method been used based on the same (15-year) recovery period. Apartment buildings actually maintain an advantage over nonresidential income property in that *all* the ACRS depreciation deduction on a nonresidential property is taxed as ordinary income, not just that portion that exceeds straight-line depreciation. The amount of recapture is limited to the extent of the gain (although the gain usually far exceeds recapture anyway). On the other hand, no recapture is taken if the straight-line method is elected, even if the property is an office building, shopping center, or other nonresidential structure. All gain is then capital gain.

The personal property recapture method used in computing the after-tax reversion is similar to that of nonresidential real property in that all gain recognized is taxed as ordinary income to the extent of prior ACRS deductions.

Example 9-2, Case Study 1.   *Computing excess depreciation and its tax.*
Total depreciation taken on a property over five years using the ACRS method is $82,800. The allowable straight-line depreciation taken over the same holding period would have been $60,000, and the investor has a 50% marginal tax rate.

Q.   What amount of tax on the excess depreciation will be deducted from the sale price in computing the net reversion?

A.

Total depreciation taken (125%)	$82,800
Allowable straight-line depreciation	(60,000)
Amount of excess depreciation	$22,800
Marginal tax rate	× 50%
Tax on excess depreciation	$11,400

The $22,800 is deducted from the net sale price along with the sale costs when computing capital gain.

Computing the Tax on Capital Gain

After excess depreciation comes the matter of computing the tax on capital gain. The capital gain itself is figured by deducting the adjusted basis (including the basis of the land), the amount of excess depreciation, and any unamortized prepaid interest (loan points) from the net sale price. The reportable portion (40%) of the gain is then multiplied by the investor's marginal tax rate to find the tax on the capital gain:

Example 9-3, Case Study 1. *Determining the capital gain and its tax.*
Using the figures computed previously in this chapter and a 50% marginal tax rate:

Q. What is the capital gain?

A.
Net sale price	$385,950
Adjusted basis	(220,200)
Excess depreciation	(22,800)
Capital gain	$142,950

Q. What is the amount of tax the investor must pay on the capital gain?

A.
% of gain reportable	× 40%
Amount of gain to be taxed	$57,180
Marginal tax rate	× 50%
Tax on capital gain	$28,590

COMPUTING THE NET REVERSION

Now that the various projected deductions from net sale price have been determined, the net reversion calculation is simple:

Example 9-4, Case Study 1. *Net reversion computation.*
Using the figures previously computed in this section and a mortgage balance of $204,849:

Q. What is the net reversion to the seller?

A.
Sale price	$415,000
Sale costs	(29,050)
Mortgage balance	(204,849)
Tax on capital gain	(28,590)
Tax on recaptured depreciation	(11,400)
Net reversion	$141,111

CHAPTER TEN

RATE OF RETURN

There are several rate of return techniques used to measure growth and return on the initial outlay. Perhaps the two most often used and discussed are the *financial management rate of return* (FMRR) and the *internal rate of return* (IRR). The concepts behind the two methods are much the same, although a presumption difference regarding the reinvestment of the cash flows will provide slightly different answers between the two. This presumption becomes less important as the cash flow pattern becomes more weighted toward the time of resale.

The financial management rate of return is used in this book to measure apartment building income, and the IRR is used for measuring lender's yield in Chapter 15. In actuality, the internal rate of return is often used to measure apartment building income as well, but preference here is given to the FMRR because it has the following attributes.

1. The FMRR can be more easily explained to a client.
2. The FMRR closely follows true life situations and decisions because of its flexible assumptions regarding reinvestment of the cash flows.
3. The FMRR does not require one of the more sophisticated calculators (Texas Instrument's Business Analyst cannot figure an internal rate of return except by repeated trial and error).
4. The internal rate of return has mathematical characteristics that occasionally result in no rate of return or two or more rates of return if the cash-flow pattern seesaws back and forth from positive to negative.

In total, the validity of both techniques is well regarded. It is ironic that, because it actually contains no cash-flow reinvestment presumptions, the IRR is more of a universal standard of comparison and is especially useful in computing the lender's yield in financing (see Chapter 15). Computing the IRR is discussed in Chapter 11. The remainder of this chapter concerns itself with the FMRR.

GROWTH AND RETURN ON MONEY

When investing money in a savings account, one expects some amount of interest and, consequently, a growth of the money over a period of time. One dollar invested in a compound interest savings account at 8% results in the following growth.

End of Year	Growth
(Start)	$1.0000
	+ 8%
1	$1.0800
	+ 8%
2	$1.1664
	+ 8%
3	$1.2597

The original $1 has grown to $1.2597 by the end of Year 3. As well as being the growth rate, the 8% figure is also the rate of return on the money.

THE FIRST YEAR'S INCOME

Now to Case Study 1. Consider what would happen if the Year 1 after-tax income of $11,015 is reinvested at an 8% annual return for five years:

Return on First Year
After-Tax Cash Flow

End of Year	Growth
1	$11,015
	+ 8%
2	$11,896
	+ 8%

End of Year	Growth
3	$12,848
	+ 8%
4	$13,876
	+ 8%
5	$14,986

The process is identical to the previous example of $1 except that the starting amount is $11,015. Since cash flows are treated as being realized at the end of the year (EOY), it is presumably reinvested at the end of Year 1 to grow in Years 2, 3, 4, and 5 at the 8% rate. After being invested at 8% for four years, the $11,015 has grown to $14,986.

Now assume all the cash flows are invested at the 8% rate. The growth of the individual cash flows can be demonstrated as follows and can be done with Calculator Procedure 3.

Cash Flow Growth at 8% Reinvestment Rate

EOY Year	Year 1 Cash Flow	Year 2 Cash Flow	Year 3 Cash Flow	Year 4 Cash Flow	Year 5 Cash Flow
1	$11,015				
	↓				
2	11,896	$10,069			
	↓	↓			
3	12,848	10,875	$10,065		
	↓	↓	↓		
4	13,876	11,744	10,870	$10,105	
	↓	↓	↓	↓	
5	14,986	12,684	11,740	10,913	$10,188

We don't need all of this, so let's take out the part we want. The sum of the fifth year totals:

$14,986 + $12,684 + $11,740 + $10,913 + $10,188 = $60,511

When each cash flow is invested upon receipt at 8% for the duration of the holding period, the ending sum totals $60,511. The net reversion can also be considered a cash flow—it is realized at the end of Year 5 along with the reinvested annual cash flows. Adding the sum of the reinvested cash flows to the net reversion results in the following amount.

$60,511 + $141,111 = $201,622

The original investment of $93,000 ($90,000 cash down plus $3,000 closing costs) has grown to a sum of $201,622 by the end of Year 5. The rate of return (FMRR) is the rate at which $93,000 must grow (compounded annually) to equal $201,622 at the end of the five periods.

By using Calculator Procedure 5, we can find the answer easily:

Rate of return = 16.74%

Proof

End of Year	Growth
Start	$ 93,000
	+ 16.74%
1	$108,566
	+ 16.74%
2	$126,737
	+ 16.74%
3	$147,950
	+ 16.74%
4	$172,714
	+ 16.74%
5	$201,622

HIGHER REINVESTMENT RATES

One of the unique characteristics of the FMRR is that the annual cash flows are reinvested at any rate the analyst sees fit. In the previous examples the cash flows were relatively small and were probably placed into a lower yield investment such as a savings account or short-term security. Up to this point we have presumed the reinvestment rate to be 8% per annum. However, if the cash flows are substantial, the investor may seek more lucrative investment opportunities, perhaps investing the money in other projects that might provide a greater rate of return.

At some point (and the analyst must decide when) there is a wealth level at which the investor can take the accumulated cash flows and reinvest them at a higher yield. Assume that this wealth level is $25,000, and the investor believes that with the proper investment one can earn a 20% rate of return instead of the 8% return characteristic of a smaller amount of funds. When the cash flows are compounded forward at 8% to a point in time when they equal $25,000 or more, they are then assumed to be reinvested to produce a higher rate of return. Meanwhile, the subsequent cash flows generated by the property in the following years are again presumed to earn 8% (while the previously reinvested cash flow is now earning 20%) until the total again reaches $25,000 (the changeover point) and the higher yield can be assumed for this set of cash flows. (Of course, the projected holding period may elapse before this event.) For example, look at an investment with the following cash flows.

End of Year	Cash Flow
(Start)	($100,000)
1	8,000
2	9,000
3	10,000
4	11,000
5	$180,000

The investor or analyst assumes that the cash flows will be reinvested to earn 8%. When the total reaches $25,000 or more, the funds will be taken from the lower yield investment and placed in another real estate project that will return 20% on the investment. Finding the year of the changeover point is a trial-and-error process and can be demonstrated using the five-year list of cash flows.

Again, assume the changeover point from an 8% to 20% yield is $25,000. The reinvested cash flows can be computed using Calculator Procedure 3. The $8,000 EOY cash flow for the first year is obviously less than $25,000, so we move onto the EOY total for the second year.

$8,000 reinvested at 8% for one year	$ 8,640
$9,000 received at the end of year 2	9,000
Total	$17,640

The $17,640 is not yet enough to reinvest at a higher rate according to the $25,000 assumption. The EOY amount for the third year is totaled.

$8,000 reinvested at 8% for two years	$ 9,331
$9,000 reinvested at 8% for one year	9,720
$10,000 received at the end of year 3	10,000
Total	$29,051

The $29,051 is a sufficient amount to reinvest at the higher 20% yield. Now the cash-flow projections and rate of return construction are:

End of Year	Cash Flow	Reinvested Amounts
(Start)	($100,000)	
1	8,000 at 8%	
2	9,000 at 8%	
3	10,000 + 9,720 + 9,331 = 29,051 at 20%	
4	11,000 at 8%	
5	$180,000 + $11,880 + $41,833 = $233,713	

Based on an initial outlay of $100,000 and a future combined value of $233,713, the rate of return is 18.51%. Note that had all the cash flow reinvestments been at the 8% rate, the return would have been 17.69%.

DIFFERENT CASH FLOW PATTERNS

So far, this chapter has only dealt with the conventional type of cash flow in which a negative initial outlay is followed by a series of positive inflows. Demonstrated in the following paragraphs are two different types of cash-flow patterns that are often encountered in real estate investments.

Negative Cash Flow in the Middle of a Holding Period

Case Study 4 has a large cash outflow in the middle of the holding period due to the renovation at the end of Year 3. The cash flows for Case Study 4 are:

End of Year	Cash Flow	
(Start)	($65,000)	
1	870	
2	1,327	
3	38	− $ 48,857 renovation costs
4	9,323	
5	$11,116	+ $256,163 reversion

There are several ways the investor could provide for the renovation cost—by refinancing, by using the investor's own funds, and so forth. In this case study, it will be assumed that the investor will set aside a sum upon purchase in anticipation of the renovation cost. The immediate question is how much money must be set aside. Cash flows for Years 1 and 2 are compounded forward (using Calculator Procedure 3 at the 8% reinvestment rate) to the time of renovation (end of Year 3) and are added to the Year 3 cash flow:

End of Year	Cash Flow	Year's Growth	Value at EOY 3
1	$ 870	2	$1,015
2	1,327	1	1,433
3	38	0	38
			$2,486

This $2,486 cash buildup can be applied toward the $48,857 renovation costs:

$$\$48,857 - \$2,486 = \$46,371$$

The $46,371 represents the shortfall, or amount of money that must be obtained from a source outside the investment itself. The task now is to determine the present value (what amount invested at the beginning of the holding period) of the eventual $46,371 shortfall. This is a substantial amount so we will assume a higher yield of 20% on this money. Using Calculator Procedure 4, we find this amount to be $26,835. In other words, $26,835 invested at 20% at time of property purchase along with the annual cash flows invested at 8% precisely total the renovation requirement. The rate of return calculation for the first three years now takes on the following format:

End of Year	Cash Flow	Year's Growth	Value at EOY 3
(Start)	($26,835)	3	$46,371
1	870	2	1,015
2	1,327	1	1,433
3	38	0	38
			$48,857

Notice that the $26,835 is treated as an outflow at the start of the investment and will be combined with the initial outlay of $65,000 when calculating the rate of return. By the end of Year 3, the cash flows generated by the investment plus the additional $26,835 invested at 20% have been offset exactly by the renovation costs. The entire holding period looks like this:

End of Year	Cash Flow	Year's Growth	Value at EOY 3
(Start)	($ 65,000)		
	($ 26,835)	3	$ 46,371
1	870	2	1,015
2	1,327	1	1,433
3	38	0	38
			$ 48,857
	($ 48,857)		renovation costs
4	9,323	1	$ 10,069
5	267,379	0	267,379
			$277,448

For computing the rate of return, the initial outlay is the cash down plus the amount set aside for renovation, which total $91,835 ($65,000 + $26,835). The final combined reversion is $286,448. Using Calculator Procedure 5, the return is found to be 25.55%.

A Series of Negative Outflows

Remember that to find the rate return (FMRR) we must first find the beginning net cash outflow and the final combined reversion. No matter what the pattern of the cash flows, these two figures must be determined to arrive at a rate of return.

Year	Cash Flow
(Start)	($10,000)
1	(10,000)
2	(10,000)
3	50,000

This pattern resembles that of a development project with a number of outflows (construction costs) followed by a large inflow (sale of project).

Assume again that the investor's safe investment rate is 8%. To find out what amount we must start out with (initial outlay), the future outflows are discounted back to the present using Calculator Procedure 4.

Year	Cash Flow	Present Values
(Start)	($10,000) + ($9,259) + ($8,573) = ($27,832)	
1	($10,000)	
2	($10,000)	

The present value of the outlays is $27,832. This amount eventually creates a net sale price of $50,000 at the end of Year 3. By again using Calculator Procedure 5, we find that the rate of return is 21.56%.

CHAPTER ELEVEN

PRESENT VALUE AND INTERNAL RATE OF RETURN

After an after-tax cash flow has been developed, another analysis application is the present value (PV) technique. Each annual cash flow is discounted back to the present (start) at the investor's required rate of return. The discounted cash flows are totaled with their sum, or present value, being the maximum initial outlay the investor can afford to pay and still receive at least the required rate of return. As discussed here, the present value is based on after-tax cash flows that accrue to the investor's equity investment. Since the property value is the total of the equity and loan positions, the loan balance can be added to the present value of the cash flows to arrive at the total property value, thus providing another method of investment valuation.

Discounting is the recriprocal function of compound interest. For example, in Chapter 10 it is demonstrated that $1.0000 left to compound itself annually at 8% becomes $1.3605 at the end of the fourth year. On the other hand, $1.3605, which is to be received four years in the future, is currently worth $1.0000 today when discounted at 8%.

SELECTION OF A DISCOUNT RATE

A key in applying the present value technique is the selection of a discount rate. The rate is based on the indicated rate of return for competitive investments with perhaps some adjustments for differences in risk, liquidity, and management (a more thorough discussion of these elements is presented

Exhibit 11-1. Compounding versus Discounting

Compounding	Discounting
$1.0000 left to grow at 8% growth rate for 4 years	$1.3605 receivable at the end of Year 4 discounted back to the present at 8%

Compounding	Discounting
$1.0000	$1.0000
↓	↑
8%	8%
↓	↑
8%	8%
↓	↑
8%	8%
↓	↑
8%	8%
↓	↑
$1.3605	$1.3605

in Chapter 12). The discount rate can be considered to be the opportunity cost of equity capital since the investment is made at the expense of foregoing another competitive investment opportunity.

If an entire investment market was composed of the four case studies in Chapter 13, an investor would be looking at an anticipated rate of return of from about 16% to 25%, depending on the amount of risk, liquidity, and management involved. However, all other investment alternatives (both real estate and nonreal estate) should be considered when choosing the discount rate. Especially interesting are *bonds* . The posted yield for a bond is really the rate at which the cash flows and reversion upon maturity are discounted back to equal the purchase price. The apartment investor certainly should expect a before-tax return above a well-rated bond due to the additional risk, non-liquidity, and management involved. On the other hand, it should be remembered that the bond yield is pretax, whereas the rate of return described herein is figured on after-tax cash flows. There is no tax shelter on corporate bonds, and the tax on income will lower the bond's true yield to the investor.

The discounting process is done with a financial calculator using Calculator Procedure 4. It is assumed that each cash flow is received at the end of its particular year.

NET PRESENT VALUE

Present value is the current value of a set of future cash flows discounted at the required rate. The sum of the discounted cash flows would only by coincidence equal the initial outlay, and any difference between the present value and the initial outlay is called the net present value (NPV). A positive NPV indicates an investment returning more than the specified rate of return, and a negative NPV warns that the cash flows are not providing the required return on the investment.

Using Case Study 1, the outcome of a 12% required return on the initial outlay is examined in the following example.

Example 11-1, Case Study 1. *Present value and net present value at a 12% return.*

Case study 1 involves an initial outlay of $93,000 and provides after-tax cash flows as listed below under the Year 1 through Year 5 columns.

The present value and net present value of the cash flows based on a 12% discount rate is calculated as in Exhibit 11-2.

A present value is excess of the initial outlay (positive NPV) indicates a return greater than the required 12% with the cash flows having an excess or net present value of $24,299. Returns appear favorable, and the investment signal is a go-ahead. The investor could put down an initial outlay of up to $117,299 and still realize a 12% return on the cash flows.

Now let's test a higher rate of return, for instance, 20%.

Exhibit 11-2.   Present Value at 12%

			Years		
Start	1	2	3	4	5
$ 9,835 ◄——— $11,015					
8,027 ◄——————— $10,069					
7,164 ◄——————————— $10,065					
6,422 ◄——————————————— $10,105					
5,781 ◄——————————————————— $ 10,188					
80,070 ◄——————————————————— $141,111					
$117,299 present value					
(93,000) initial outlay					
$ 24,299 net present value					

Example 11-2, Case Study 1.   *Present value and net present value at a 20% rate of return.*

The initial cash outlay and cash flows are the same as those cited in the previous example.

The present value and the net present value based on a 20% discount rate are calculated as in Exhibit 11-3.

A present value of less than the initial outlay (negative NPV) indicates that the investment cannot generate the 20% rate of return required, and a purchase based on this parameter is inadvisable.

Further leveraging of this investment through the use of a larger loan and less down payment would help increase the return of the investment. Decreasing the initial outlay by $5,328 would result in the cash flows generating the 20% rate of return. In actuality, however, it is usually not that simple, because an increase in the loan means a corresponding decrease in the cash flows due to possible changes in depreciation and loan payments, and the 20% requirement may still not be met.

INTERNAL RATE OF RETURN (IRR)

The IRR is the rate that discounts the cash flows to equal the initial outlay precisely (a zero NPV). The IRR for the cash flows cited here is 18.31%.

Exhibit 11-3.   Present Value at 20%

			Years		
Start	1	2	3	4	5
$ 9,179 ◄——— $11,015					
6,992 ◄——————— $10,069					
5,825 ◄——————————— $10,065					
4,873 ◄————————————————— $10,105					
4,094 ◄——————————————————————— $ 10,188					
56,709 ◄——————————————————————— $141,111					

$87,672   present value

(93,000)   initial outlay

($ 5,328)   net present value

Without the use of a financial calculator, the IRR calculation involves the trial and error of various rates until the perfectly balanced initial outlay present value (zero NPV) relationship is reached.

Aside from the actual arithmetic involved, the basic difference between the IRR and FMRR is that the IRR presumes a reinvestment of the cash flows at the internal rate of return itself, whereas the FMRR assumes that the cash flows are reinvested at a specified rate. If the FMRR reinvestment rate was the same as the IRR, their computations would yield the same rate.

If, when computing a present value , net present value, or IRR, a negative cash flow is encountered, the negative amount is discounted back to the present and (as a negative) is deducted from rather than added to the summation of the cash flows.

CHAPTER TWELVE

DECISION MAKING

Having computed the rate of return for the different investment alternatives, one might think that the selection process is as easy as selecting the opportunity indicating the best return. However, the elements of *risk, liquidity, and management* have not been included in the cash flow or rate of return computations. These items are all substantial factors in the ownership of apartment buildings, and each must be considered in regard to the investor/property relationship that will take place if the particular alternative is chosen.

RISK

It is inevitable that the actual performance of the investment will vary somewhat from the projections, and a degree of risk is always present when the amount or direction of the variances are not known. The following paragraphs outline the risks that must be considered.

1. Changes in market trends, population trends, demographics, and economics can change rent levels and expenses as well as supply/demand factors at time of resale.

2. A building might show an adequate rate of return but might also be especially susceptible to governmental actions such as rent control, condemnation, zone changes, and changes in tax laws.

3. Little can be done to thwart exterior nuisances such as neighborhood decline, visual blight, noise, and odors.

4. Excessive costs due to the unforeseen failure of structural and mechanical systems or casualty losses are not figured into the cash-flow projection.

5. A financial risk is undertaken when the investment is heavily leveraged and loan payments are so high that they jeopardize the ability of the investor to meet payments.

These risks have *not* been factored into the cash flow or rate of return projections, but they must be recognized and analyzed in relation to the risk-bearing capabilities of the investor and the indicated rate of return. A small investor with all the eggs in one basket is not in a position to carry the same risks as the more wealthy investor, but indications of higher returns are certainly an inducement to take on additional risk. On the other hand, a marginal rate of return coupled with substantial risk is the wrong combination.

No investment is safe from risk. Even if cash is kept and no investment made, a substantial risk exists in the probable reduction of purchasing power through inflation. Different types and amounts of risk are associated with different types of investments, and, to a lesser degree, each apartment building investment is subject to risk combinations peculiar to it alone.

LIQUIDITY

Liquidity is a measure of an investment's ability to be converted into cash. The more liquid the investment, the easier it can be converted into cash in a reasonable period of time without the sacrifice of sale price or terms.

Liquidity is desirable because of occasional and unexpected cash needs as well as the possibilities of encountering more profitable investment opportunities in the future. Since it, too, is based on uncertainties, it is really another form of risk.

Real estate ranks poor in liquidity compared to other investments, but should compensate by providing a greater return. A single-family house is usually the most liquid form of real estate because of continued demand and the availability of financing. Apartment buildings (depending mostly on the financing market) often rank second, ahead of office buildings, industrial properties and raw land. Special use properties can be very difficult to withdraw equity dollars from.

Availability of financing has perhaps the strongest effect on liquidity. You can give a building away, but obtaining the best sale price at reasonable terms in a short amount of time generally requires a source of financing. If the seller must provide financing, there will still be a lack of liquidity. There should be an outside source of funds for an investment to be liquid, most often from an institutional lender such as a savings and loan organization, bank, pension fund, or insurance company.

Smaller buildings are usually easier to finance, but there is no set answer to the question of which type of apartment building will afford the greatest availability of financing. Depending on their mood, lenders may favor pride-of-ownership buildings on one occasion and older bread-and-butter buildings with larger cash flows on other occasions. Liquidity is also dependent on the form of ownership. A joint ownership often results in funds being committed for an uncertain and uncontrollable length of time, causing interim investment opportunities to be lost.

An assessment of the investor's liquidity needs should be made prior to the search for an investment with some of the available funds withheld as needed. If an investment looks like a good performer but is so sizable that it seriously impairs the investor's reserves, it should receive an extra critical look and provide some additional compensation to boost the return or lessen the risk.

MANAGEMENT

In an optimal situation, with on-site and professional management, the investor has only to sit back and collect a check at the end of the year with no mental or physical exertion at all. Headaches will persist, however, and there probably will be some time requirement, which could range from accounting duties all the way to a complete renovation project or other management intensive situation requiring a full-time commitment.

The smaller the investor and property, the more likely that the investor will personally perform most or all of the management duties. The larger the investor and property, the more likely that management services will be hired or contracted to afford time for the investor to concentrate on other concerns. Also, proximity of the property to the investor's home operation is another consideration in how the property is to be managed.

SCENARIOS

An optional approach to dealing with risk, liquidity, and management considerations is to make additional projections or a sensitivity analysis based on different sets of occurrences. So far the case studies have been projected according to the most probable expectations. It may be advisable to make additional projections based on both pessimistic and optimistic scenarios within the realm of reasonable possibility.

For instance, if after making the initial projection we consider it also possible that expenses may increase at an even greater pace, we can reproject using a higher growth rate for expenses. If we want to find out what will happen if demand drops and/or financing tightens, we can decrease the reversion.

To give an example using Case Study 1, assume the investor wants to know how sensitive the rates of return will be based on both a more conservative projection and a more optimistic projection. The projection changes that will be assumed for each scenario are:

Projection Changes for Case Study 1

Projection	Annual Income Growth	Annual Expense Growth	Overall Rate at Resale
Pessimistic	8.5% (No change)	15% (Up 3%)	9.5% (Up 1.18%)
Optimistic	12% (Up 3.5%)	12% (No change)	7.75% (Down 0.57%)

Calculations won't be as tedious as they are for the original projections because depreciation, interest, and mortgage balances will remain the same. The tax payable/tax savings, after-tax cash flow, reversion, and rate of return are recalculated to reflect the new annual net income and resale reversion. The original projection along with the two new projections and their rates of return are:

Projection	Annual Income Growth	Annual Expense Growth	Overall Rate at Resale	Annual Rate of Return (FMRR)
Pessimistic	8.5%	15.0%	9.50%	7.90%
Most probable	8.5	12.0	8.32	16.74
Optimistic	12.0	12.0	7.75	28.77

Based on the three projections that reflect our respective expectations, we have a very good chance of realizing at least the pessimistic projection of a 7.90% rate of return; about an even chance of getting the most probable return of 16.74%, and, if things swing in our favor, the investment might provide the 28.77% optimistic rate.

The pessimistic projection reflects the least risk since the investment has to perform only at minimal expectations to achieve the 7.90% return. There is a smaller chance of realizing the optimistic projection, and basing a decision heavily on this scenario would certainly provide more risk.

USING THE PRESENT VALUE TECHNIQUE

A decision on whether to purchase or become involved in an intensive management situation might be handled through the present value technique. As an example, look at Case Studies 3 and 4. Both involve the same building purchased at the same terms. The difference comes at the end of Year 3 of the five-year holding period when the Case Study 4 building undergoes an extensive renovation with a corresponding increase in annual cash flows and value at that time. However, the renovation will cause a short-term but heavy management commitment on the part of the investor who plans on personally contracting and supervising the work.

If the initial outlays for each case study were the same, the cash flows would be discounted back to the present with the difference between the present values attributable to the additional management burdens of renovation; however, the initial outlay in Case Study 4 is effectively $26,835 higher because this amount was invested separately upon purchase at a 20% return to make up for the projected shortfall in renovation funding (for the calculation methodology, see Chapter 10). Since the $26,835 is an outflow at the very beginning of the investment, it is deducted in whole (without discounting) from the present value of the cash flows for Case Study 4. The reinvested Year 1, 2, and 3 cash flows were also pulled back into the investment and applied toward the renovation costs. Therefore, with the cash flows reinvested and consequently used to offset renovation costs, we will assume no cash flow to the investor until Years 4 and 5.

Both Case Studies 3 and 4 are discounted at the same rate (which assumes the same risk and liquidity considerations for each alternative) with the

Exhibit 12-1.   Case Study 3 Present Value Calculation

Present Value	Annual Cash Flows				
	1	2	3	4	5
$ 737 ◄——$870					
953 ◄————$1,327					
1,108 ◄—————$1,821					
873 ◄——————$1,693					
1,010 ◄———————$ 2,311					
60,632 ◄———————$138,712					
$65,313 present value					

Exhibit 12-2.   Case Study 4 Present Value Calculation

Present Value	Annual Cash Flows				
	1	2	3	4	5
$ 0	*				
0		*			
0			*		
4,809				$9,323	
4,859					$ 11,116
112,015					$256,263
$121,683					
(26,835)	Additional outlay to fund EOY 3 renovation				
$ 94,848	Present value				

*First three years' cash flows have already been discounted to cover the renovation.

discount rate reflecting the investor's rate of return expectations. Assume this rate is 18%. The cash flows are discounted in Exhibits 12-1 and 12-2.

The difference between the two present values is $29,535 in favor of Case Study 4. This is the present value of the cash-flow increase attributable to the Case Study 4 renovation, or what the investor has earned through additional management efforts. The decision whether the extra $29,535 makes it worthwhile to renovate is left to the investor.

CASH-FLOW TIMING

If the investor is on a tight budget and is stretching to meet payments, an especially hard look should be taken at the cash-flow timing. As an example, consider the before- and after-tax cash flows for Case Study 2:

Year	1	2	3	4	5
Before-tax cash flow	($3,266)	($1,459)	$ 446	$2,452	$4,559
After-tax cash flow	8,765	7,819	7,815	7,855	7,938

The investor's first year's budgeting for meeting expense and loan servicing requirements should be based on the before-tax cash flow rather than the after-tax since the ATCF includes a tax shelter benefit that is not realized until tax return time the following year.

CONCLUSION

After the rates of return and/or present values are calculated for the different alternatives, the final step is to reconcile all the considerations into a final decision.

The decision will rest heavily on which alternative offers the best numbers, but the reliability of the data used in each analysis must still be considered acceptable, and the analyst should also find the projections comfortably realistic. The profile of the investor should be considered in relation to the characteristics of the investment with the chosen alternative maximizing the investor's wealth but not at the cost of creating precarious risk, liquidity, or management situations.

CHAPTER THIRTEEN

CASE STUDIES

This chapter presents four case studies—two properties with two sets of assumptions for each one.

Case Study 1. A 12-unit, 15-year-old apartment building purchased with a 70% loan and 30% cash down.

Case Study 2. This is the same property presented in Case Study 1 but with the seller carrying back a second mortgage for 15% of sale price and the cash down payment correspondingly reduced to 15%.

Case Study 3. This is an older, furnished building.

Case Study 4. This is the Case Study 3 property but with an extensive renovation planned for the end of the third year.
A list of pertinent assumptions is provided at the beginning of each case study. Then the necessary computations leading to the indicated rate of return are provided. No purchase decision is suggested because this depends on the individual investor and how the investor perceives the different risk, liquidity, and management factors.

CASE STUDY 1—ASSUMPTIONS AND PROJECTIONS

PROPERTY   12 units, 15-year-old, side walk-up in average
                      area.

PURCHASE PRICE $300,000.

CASH DOWN $90,000 plus $3,000 closing costs incidental to the sale.

LOAN $210,000 first mortgage at 11.75%, 30-year amortization, monthly payments. Annual payment is $25,437.

INCOME $36,691 effective gross income (at purchase) increasing at 8.5% per year with the first increase effective at the end of Year 1.

EXPENSES $11,731 per year (at purchase) increasing 12% per year. First increase effective at the end of Year 1.

DEPRECIATION   Use ACRS 15-year depreciation schedule. Improvements represent 60% of the total value.

RESALE   Investment to sell at same overall rate that it was purchased at (8.32%). Sale costs are 7%.

TAX RATE   Investor has a 50% marginal tax rate.

STRATEGY   Maintain property in present condition and sell at the end of five years.

RATE OF RETURN   Financial management rate of return. Cash-flow reinvestment rate is 8% per annum.

Exhibit 13-1. Income and Expense Schedule

Income	
4 (2-1) @ $300 per month	$ 1,200
8 (1-1) @ $240 per month	1,920
	3,120
	× 12
Annual gross income	$37,440
Less: Vacancy and collection loss @ 2%	749
Effective gross annual income	$36,691

Expenses	
Fixed	
Property taxes	$ 3,750
Insurance	504
Operating	
Gas	592
Electric	175
Water	555
Repairs, maintenance, and decorating	2,568
Gardening	420
Refuse	333
Management	734
Reserves	
Stoves (6 @ $240/5 years)	288
Refrigerators (6 @ $250/5 years)	300
Disposals (12 @ $55/5 years)	132
Carpets and drapes (all units/5 years)	1,380
Total expenses	(11,731)
Net operating income	$24,960

Exhibit 13-2.   Income and Expense Growth

End of Year	Income Growth @ 8.5%	Expense Growth @ 12%	NOI
(Start)	$36,691	$11,371	$24,960
1	39,810	13,139	26,671
2	43,194	14,716	28,478
3	46,865	16,482	30,383
4	50,849	18,460	32,389
5	55,171	20,675	34,496

Exhibit 13-3.   Interest and Amortization Schedule

End of Year	EOY Loan Balance	Amortization	Interest
(Start)	$210,000		
1	209,196	$ 804	$24,633
2	208,292	903	24,534
3	207,276	1,016	24,421
4	206,132	1,143	24,294
5	204,849	1,284	24,153

Exhibit 13-4.   Real Property Depreciation Schedule

Year	Depreciable Basis	Depreciation Factor	Depreciation Allowance
1	$180,000	12%	$21,600
2	180,000	10	18,000
3	180,000	9	16,200
4	180,000	8	14,400
5	180,000	7	12,600

EOY 5 adjusted basis = $220,200
Recaptured depreciation = $22,800

Exhibit 13-5. Taxable Income

Tax Savings or Tax Payable

Year	1	2	3	4	5
NOI	$26,671	$28,478	$30,383	$32,389	$34,496
Mortgage interest	(24,633)	(24,534)	(24,421)	(24,294)	(24,153)
Depreciation	(21,600)	(18,000)	(16,200)	(14,400)	(12,600)
Taxable income	(19,562)	(14,056)	(10,238)	(6,305)	(2,257)
Marginal tax rate	0.50	0.50	0.50	0.50	0.50
Tax savings	$ 9,781	$ 7,028	$ 5,119	$ 3,153	$ 1,129
Tax payable	—	—	—	—	—

After-Tax Cash Flow

	1	2	3	4	5
NOI	$26,671	$28,478	$30,383	$32,389	$34,496
Loan payments	(25,437)	(25,437)	(25,437)	(25,437)	(25,437)
Before-tax cash flow	1,234	3,041	4,946	6,952	9,059
Tax savings	9,781	7,028	5,119	3,153	1,129
Tax payable	—	—	—	—	—
After-tax cash flow	$11,015	$10,069	$10,065	$10,105	$10,188

Exhibit 13-6.   Net Reversion

Tax on Excess Depreciation

Total depreciation taken	$ 82,800
Allowable straight-line depreciation	(60,000)
Excess depreciation	22,800
Marginal tax rate	0.50
Tax on excess depreciation	$ 11,400

Tax on Capital Gain

	$415,000
Sale costs	(29,050)
Net sales price	$385,950
Adjusted basis	(220,200)
Excess depreciation	(22,800)
Capital gain	$142,950
% gain reportable	0.40
Amount of gain taxed	57,180
Marginal tax rate	0.50
Tax on Capital gain	$ 28,590

Net Reversion

Sale price	$415,000
Sale costs	(29,050)
Mortgage balance	(204,849)
Tax on capital gain	(28,590)
Tax on excess depreciation	(11,400)
Net reversion	$141,111

Exhibit 13-7.   Rate of Return

Year	After-Tax Cash Flow	Year's Growth	ATCF Future Value Reinvested @ 8%
Start	$(93,000)		
1	11,015	4	$ 14,986
2	10,069	3	12,684
3	10,065	2	11,740
4	10,105	1	10,913
5	10,188	0	10,188
5	141,111	0	141,111 (reversion)
			$201,622

Initial outlay	($93,000)
Future value	$201,622
Rate of return	16.74%

CASE STUDY 2—ASSUMPTIONS AND PROJECTIONS

All assumptions and projections for Case Study 2 are the same as those in Case Study 1 except that the seller carries back a second mortgage and the downpayment is thereby reduced.

Modifications

Cash down	$45,000
Second loan	$45,000 at 10% interest, payable interest only, all due in five years. Annual payment = $4,500.

NOTE.   Only items changed due to the inclusion of the second mortgage are shown. Items that will not change from Case Study 1 are omitted or noted with an asterisk.

Exhibit 13-8. Interest and Amortization Schedule

Year	BOY Loan Balance (First)	Amortization on First	First Mortgage Interest	Second Mortgage Interest	Total Interest
1	*	*	*	$4,500	$29,133
2	*	*	*	4,500	29,034
3	*	*	*	4,500	28,921
4	*	*	*	4,500	28,794
5	*	*	*	4,500	28,653

Exhibit 13-9. Taxable Income

			Tax Savings or Tax Payable		
Year	1	2	3	4	5
NOI	*	*	*	*	*
Mortgage interest	$(29,133)	$(29,034)	$(28,921)	$(28,794)	$(28,653)
Depreciation	(*)	(*)	(*)	(*)	(*)
Taxable income	(24,062)	(18,556)	(14,738)	(10,805)	(6,757)
Marginal tax rate	*	*	*	*	*
Tax savings	$ 12,031	$ 9,278	$ 7,369	$ 5,403	$ 3,379
Tax payable	—	—	—	—	—

Exhibit 13-10. After-Tax Cash Flow

Year	1	2	3	4	5
NOI	*	*	*	*	*
Loan payments					
First Mortgage	(*)	(*)	(*)	(*)	(*)
Second Mortgage	$ (4,500)	$ (4,500)	$ (4,500)	$ (4,500)	$ (4,500)
Before-tax cash flow	(3,226)	(1,459)	446	2,452	4,559
Tax savings	12,031	9,278	7,369	5,403	3,379
tax payable	—	—	—	—	—
After-tax cash flow	$ 8,765	$ 7,819	$ 7,815	$ 7,855	$ 7,938

Exhibit 13-11. Net Reversion

Sale Price	$ *
Sale Costs	(*)
Mortgage balance	
first	(*)
second	(45,000)
Tax on capital gain	(*)
Tax on excess depreciation	(*)
Net reversion	$ 96,111

Exhibit 13-12. Rate of Return

Year	After-tax Cash Flow	Year's Growth	ATCF Future Value Reinvested @ 8%
Start	($48,000)		
1	$8,765	4	$ 11,925
2	7,819	3	9,850
3	7,815	2	9,115
4	7,855	1	8,483
5	7,938	0	7,938
5	96,111	0	96,111 (reversion)
			$143,422

Initial outlay	$ (48,000)
Future value	$ 143,422
Rate of return	24.47%

CASE STUDY 3—ASSUMPTIONS AND PROJECTIONS

PROPERTY	18 units, 40-year-old, center-hall plan building in fair condition. All units are furnished singles (living room and kitchen).
PURCHASE PRICE	$250,000
CASH DOWN	$62,500 plus $2,500 closing costs incidental to the sale.
LOANS	
first	$162,500 first mortgage at 12.00%, 25-year amortization, monthly payments. Annual payment is $20,538.

second	$25,000 second mortgage at 10% per annum interest, payable interest only, all due in five years. Annual payment is $2,500.
INCOME	$32,141 effective gross income (at purchase) increasing at 10.0% per year with the first increase effective at the end of Year 1.
EXPENSES	$14,659 per year (at purchase) increasing 12% per year. First increase effect at the end of Year 1
DEPRECIATION	Use ACRS 15-year depreciation schedule. Improvements represent 20% of the total value. Personal property represents 1.5% purchase price. Use ACRS 1981–1984 depreciation schedule with a three-year life.
RESALE	Investment to sell at same overall rate that it was purchased at (6.99%). Sale costs are 7%.
TAX RATE	Investor has a 50% marginal tax rate.
STRATEGY	Maintain property in present condition and sell at the end of five years. No replacement of personal property.
RATE OF RETURN	Financial management rate of return. Cash flow reinvestment rate is 8% per annum.

Exhibit 13-13.   Income and Expense Schedule

Income	
18 furnished singles @ $155/month	$ 2,790
	× 12
Annual gross income	$33,480
Less Vacancy and Collection Loss @ 4%	1,339
Effective gross annual income	$32,141
Expenses	
Fixed	
property taxes	$ 3,125
insurance	718
Operating	
gas	990
electric	1,317
water	468

Exhibit 13-13. *(Continued)*

Expenses

repair, maintenance, and decorating	2,732
gardening	360
refuse	333
professional management	1,286
resident manager	2,250
Reserves:	
carpets and drapes	$ 1,080
Total expenses	$14,659
Net operating income	$17,482

Exhibit 13-14.   Income and Expense Growth

End of Year	Income Growth @ 10%	Expense Growth @ 12%	NOI
(Start)	$32,141	$14,659	$17,482
1	35,355	16,418	18,937
2	38,891	18,388	20,503
3	42,780	20,595	22,185
4	47,058	23,066	23,992
5	51,763	25,834	25,929

Exhibit 13-15. Interest and Amortization Schedule

Year	BOY Loan Balance (First)	Amortization on First	First Mortgage Interest	Second Mortgage Interest	Total Interest
1	$162,500	$1,097	$19,441	$2,500	$21,941
2	161,403	1,236	19,302	2,500	21,802
3	160,167	1,393	19,145	2,500	21,645
4	158,774	1,569	18,969	2,500	21,469
5	157,205	1,768	18,770	2,500	21,270

Exhibit 13-16.   Real Property Depreciation Schedule

Year	Depreciable Basis	Depreciation Factor	Depreciation Allowance
1	$50,000	12%	$6,000
2	50,000	10	5,000
3	50,000	9	4,500
4	50,000	8	4,000
5	50,000	7	3,500

EOY 5 adjusted basis = $229,500
Recaptured depreciation = $6,333

Exhibit 13-17.   Personal Property Depreciation Schedule

Year	Depreciable Basis	Depreciation Factor	Annual Depreciation
1	$3,750	25%	$ 938
2	3,750	38	1,425
3	3,750	37	1,387

EOY 5 adjusted basis = 0
Recaptured depreciation = $3,750

Exhibit 13-18. Taxable Income

Tax Savings or Tax Payable

Year	1	2	3	4	5
NOI	$18,937	$20,503	$22,185	$23,992	$25,929
Mortgage interest	(21,941)	(21,802)	(21,645)	(21,469)	(21,270)
Depreciation	(6,938)	(6,425)	(5,887)	(4,000)	(3,500)
Taxable income	(9,942)	(7,724)	(5,347)	(1,477)	(1,159)
Marginal tax rate	0.50	0.50	0.50	0.50	0.50
Tax savings	$ 4,971	$ 3,862	$ 2,674		
Tax payable				$ 739	$ 580

After-Tax Cash Flow

Year	1	2	3	4	5
NOI	$18,937	$20,503	$22,185	$23,992	$25,929
Loan payments	(23,038)	(23,038)	(23,038)	(23,038)	(23,038)
Before-tax cash flow	(4,101)	(2,535)	(853)	954	2,891
Tax savings	4,971	3,862	2,674	—	—
Tax payable	—	—	—	739	580
After-tax cash flow	$ 870	$ 1,327	$ 1,821	$ 1,693	$ 2,311

Exhibit 13-19. Net Reversion

Tax on Excess Depreciation	
Total depreciation taken	$ 26,750
Allowable straight-line depreciation	(16,667)
Excess depreciation	$ 10,083
Marginal tax rate	0.50
Tax on excess depreciation	$ 5,042

Tax on Capital Gain	
Sale price	$371,000
Sale costs	(25,970)
Net sale price	$345,030
Adjusted basis	(225,750)
Excess depreciation	(10,803)
Capital gain	$108,477
% gain reportable	0.40
Amount of gain taxed	$ 43,391
Marginal tax rate	0.50
Tax on capital gain	$ 21,695

Net Reversion	
Sale price	$371,000
Sale costs	(25,970)
Mortgage balances	(180,437)
Tax on capital gain	(21,695)
Tax on excess depreciation	(5,042)
Net reversion	$137,856

Exhibit 13-20. Rate of Return

Year	After-Tax Cash Flow	Year's Growth	ATCF Future Value Reinvested @ 8%
Start	$(65,000)		
1	870	4	$ 1,184
2	1,327	3	1,672
3	1,821	2	2,214
4	1,693	1	1,828
5	2,311	0	2,311
5	138,712	0	137,856 (reversion)
			$147,065

Initial outlay	$(65,000)
Future value	$147,831
Rate of return	17.74

CASE STUDY 4—ASSUMPTIONS AND PROJECTIONS

All assumptions and projections for Case Study 4 are the same as those in Case Study 3 except that a renovation of the property is assumed at the end of Year 3.

Modifications

Renovation Cost

Real property

18 units carpeting	$ 6,120
18 units kitchen and bath flooring	2,700
18 units kitchen and bath remodeling	4,500
18 units paint	1,620
paint hallways	300
carpet hallways, 130 yards	1,008
miscellaneous	2,000

Current cost of real property renovation	$18,248
12% per annum inflation factor	× 1.40
Projected cost of real property renovation	$25,547

Personal property

18 units furniture	$ 7,650
18 stoves and refrigerators	9,000

Current cost of personal property	$16,650
12% per annum inflation factor	× 1.40
Projected cost of real property	$23,310
Total renovation cost	$48,857

Renovation	Renovation costs are considered to be a capital improvement and are added to the adjusted basis rather than expensed.
Income	Assume loss of one month's income due to renovation time. Income to increase $45 per month per unit due to renovation. Increase to be effective BOY 4.
Resale	Overall rate for computing disposition price to be reduced to 7.00% due to additional pride of ownership.

NOTE. Only items changed due to the inclusion of the second mortgage are shown. Items that will not change from Case Study 3 are omitted or noted with an asterisk.

Exhibit 13-21.   Income and Expense Growth

End of Year	Income Growth @ 8.5%	Expense Growth @ 12%	NOI
(Start)	*	*	*
1	*	*	*
2	*	*	*
3	$39,215	*	$18,620
		Renovation	
4	$56,778	*	$33,712
5	62,456	*	36,622

Exhibit 13-22.   Real Property Depreciation Schedule

Year	Depreciable Basis	Depreciation Factor	Depreciation Allowance
1	*	*	*
2	*	*	*
3	*	*	*
4	$75,547	*	$6,044
5	75,547	*	5,288

EOY 5 Adjusted Basis = $251,215
Recaptured depreciation = $6,759

Exhibit 13-23.   Personal Property Depreciation Schedule

Year	Depreciable Basis	Depreciation Factor	Annual Depreciation
1	*	*	*
2	*	*	*
3	*	*	*
		Renovation	
4	$23,310	15%	$3,497
5	23,310	22	5,128

EOY 5 adjusted basis = $14,685
Recaptured depreciation = $12,375

Exhibit 13-24. Taxable Income

Tax Savings or Tax Payable

Year	1	2	3	4	5
NOI	*	*	$18,620	$33,712	$36,622
Mortgage interest			*	(*)	(*)
Depreciation	*	*	*	(9,541)	(10,416)
Taxable income	*	*	(8,912)	2,702	4,936
Marginal tax rate	*	*	*	*	*
Tax savings			$ 4,456	$ 1,351	$ 2,468
Tax payable	—	—	—	—	—

After-tax Cash Flow

	1	2	3	4	5
NOI	*	*	*	*	*
Loan payments	*	*	*	*	*
Before-tax cash flow	*	*	$(4,418)	$10,674	$13,584
Tax savings	*	*	4,456		
Tax payable after-tax				(1,351)	(2,468)
After-tax cash flow	*	*	$ 38	$ 9,323	$11,116

Exhibit 13-25. Net Reversion

Tax on Excess Depreciation

Total real property depreciation	$ 26,832
Allowable straight-line depreciation	(20,073)
Real property recaptured depreciation	$ 6,759
Total personal property depreciation	$ 12,375
Total recaptured depreciation	$ 19,134
Marginal tax rate	0.50
Tax on excess depreciation	$ 9,567

Tax on Capital Gain

Sale price	$524,000
Sale costs	(36,680)
Net sale price	$487,320
Adjusted basis	(262,150)
Recaptured depreciation	(19,134)
Capital gain	$206,036
% gain reportable	0.40
Amount of gain taxed	$ 82,414
Marginal tax rate	0.50
Tax on capital gain	

Exhibit 13-25. *(Continued)*

Net Reversion	
Sale price	$524,000
Sale costs	(36,680)
Mortgage balances	(*)
Tax on capital gain	(41,207)
Tax on excess depreciation	(9,567)
Net reversion	$256,263

Exhibit 13-26. Rate of Return

Year	After-Tax Cash Flow	Year's Growth	ATCF Future Value Reinvested @ 8%
Start	($65,000)		
	($26,835)		$ 46,371*
1	870	2	1,015
2	1,327	1	1,433
3	38	0	38
	Renovation		$ 48,857†
4	$ 9,323	1	10,069
5	11,116	0	11,116
5	265,263	0	256,263 (reversion)
			$277,448

Initial outlay	$(91,835)
Future value	$277,448
Rate of return	24.75%

*The $46,371 has been reinvested at 20% rather than 8%.
†The total of the reinvested cash flows up to the end of Year 3 equal the renovation costs.

PART THREE

FINANCING

CHAPTER FOURTEEN

FINANCE

When money is tight, the apartment building market is drastically affected. However, this very fact was responsible for the birth and growth of creative financing—now a tradition with apartment building sales and fast becoming a way of life for single-family residential and commercial properties. Not only does finance have a bearing on the quantity of transactions, but it also has a tremendous influence on the investor's return. Sale prices can soar if the financing is favorable or make the property extremely difficult to sell if it isn't.

So many different financing structures have been used in apartment sales that any attempt to describe the possibilities certainly would be shortsighted. However, this chapter does present many of the basic instruments and techniques upon which financing and creative financing are built. Note that many high volume institutional lenders market only standard loan packages but may be amenable to your custom structured package if the yield meets their requirements.

INSTITUTIONAL LENDERS

Institutional lenders are closely regulated by the state or federal government and obtain their funds through a banking, savings, or insurance institution. These include commercial banks, mutual savings banks, savings and loan associations, and life insurance companies.

Institutional lenders may transact loans using their own staff, or they may rely on an independent entity to help originate and/or service the loans.

These outside firms are mortgage brokers, mortgage bankers, and mortgage correspondents.

A mortgage broker is one who finds the borrower, gets the loan application, and presents the package to the lender. The mortgage banker provides the same services that the mortgage broker does but may also invest its own capital in a mortgage, even if it is only for an interim period prior to an institutional lender's purchase of the loan. The mortgage banker may also service the loan for the institution, collecting payments, making periodic inspections, and so forth. A mortgage correspondent is either a mortgage broker or mortgage banker contracted by an institution. The contract may cover subjects such as the correspondent's fee for servicing loans and the minimum business volume that the correspondent must generate to maintain the relationship.

Within the institution itself there are a number of functions that are handled by different people. There are usually two major management divisions: one for the savings, banking, or insurance function and another for the company's investment of these receipts. The real estate department might be a part of a larger division that includes other investments. The person in charge of the real estate division oversees a number of functions that could include underwriting, appraisal, loan origination, loan closing, project inspection, and legal matters.

The lender may or may not have a separate apartment building department division. Apartments most probably will be under the same jurisdiction that other income producing properties are. When contacting the lender (in the absence of a mortgage broker), one usually talks to a person with the title of loan officer, loan agent, or loan consultant. This individual could be working on a commission basis and is responsible for creating business and bringing the loan package (appraisal, credit report, loan application, and other required documents) to the loan committee.

The loan committee may consist of either a number of high level people in the company or only one person. The committee reviews the documentation on the property and borrower and makes the decision whether to lend and on what terms and conditions. The document that tells the committee about the property is the appraisal report, which is done by either an in-house appraiser or an independent fee appraiser. Once the loan is approved, the documentation goes to a loan closing or escrow secretary. This person acts as a collector and checkpoint, making sure that all the required conditions for funding are met. These conditions might include the receipt of a satisfactory termite report, title insurance policy, survey, assignment of rents, and certificate of occupancy. Most important, this person sees to the signing of the mortgage or deed of trust and its note and makes sure the proper documents are recorded with the county recorder at the date of funding.

After the loan funds, the servicing of the loan (including payment collections, payoffs, prepayment penalties, and notifications) is handled by the loan servicing department.

STANDARD FIRST MORTGAGES

A standard first loan is that usually made by an institutional lender and gives the lender a first claim on the security in case of default. Most apartment building loans made by institutional lenders are conventional loans as opposed to loans guaranteed or insured by governmental agencies such as FHA.

Once heavily dependent on this type of loan, the apartment building investment has steadily been forced to move toward other financing sources because of tightened money availability and lenders' refusals to underwrite such loans at terms necessary to make the investments pencil out. However, many apartment buildings still have one of these loans intact from times past, usually at a favorable interest rate but at a less favorable loan-to-value ratio. Hence resales often find the purchaser assuming or taking title subject to one of these underlying loans with some portion of the remaining sale price financed creatively. Standard first mortgages made on apartments are usually on newly constructed properties or at loan-to-value ratios substantially below the one-time norm of 75% or 80%.

ALTERNATIVE MORTGAGE INSTRUMENTS

Alternative mortgage instruments (AMIS) are variations of the standard conventional loan and are designed to boost real estate lending activity by offering mortgage terms appetizing to both lenders and borrowers. Because of the ever-changing policies administered to the state and federal chartered lending institutions, it is sometimes difficult to keep abreast of who is allowed to offer what. However, the use of AMIS is almost monopolized by institutional lenders. For the borrower, a discounted cash-flow analysis will give an indication of whether an AMIS is a profitable alternative to other forms of available financing.

The *variable-rate mortgage* (VRM) has an interest rate that can be adjusted periodically upward or downward depending on the movement of a cost-of-funds index. This index could be tied to the prime rate, bond yield, a passbook rate, or the index published by the Federal Home Loan Bank. The VRM permits lending institutions to maintain a spread between their borrowing and lending costs. With a straight-rate mortgage this spread often can be out of synchronization due to an institution's pattern of borrowing short and lending long. To keep pace with the index, payments may increase, decrease, or remain fixed with the loan term increasing or decreasing to accommodate the fluctuation of the index.

Rollover mortgages are fixed-rate mortgages that have payments based on typical amortization periods even though the rate is renegotiated at specific intervals, typically every five years. This concept is similar to the VRM but allows fixed payments for a longer period of time and does away with the rate index.

Shared appreciation mortgages (SAM) allow the lender to charge less interest in anticipation of sharing a percentage of the appreciation profits once the property sells or is refinanced. This may be an unsatisfactory arrangement for the apartment investor who buys at a small or negative cash flow and whose return is largely predicated on resale proceeds. A discounted cash-flow analysis is a must for any borrower who wishes to make an informed decision.

With the shared appreciation mortgage, the lender will often demand its ownership share at a predetermined time. If the property has not yet been sold, it must be appraised to find its value increase and then refinanced to compensate the lender. This arrangement is not without risk, since a tight money market could mean that the refinancing could only be done at ruinous terms. Even if terms are reasonable, the lender risks poor public relations in demanding that the owner refinance. Also, under the terms required by the lender, the borrower may not be allowed to refinance the property prior to the time that the lender is to share in the appreciation. Upon finally sharing in the appreciation, the lender has no guarantee as to what the tax consequences will be at the time—whether the shared appreciation will be treated as additional interest or as a long-term capital gain.

PARTICIPATION LOANS

After spending years on the sidelines watching their borrowers reap the fruits of ownership-associated upsides (increases in income and value), lenders have finally become interested in sharing the benefits and are doing so through participation loans. This is simply a loan that allows the lender a share of the property's gross income, net income, or after-debt service income. Whatever the type of income the lender participates in, the participation (also known as an equity kicker) is usually based on either a fixed percent of the income or on any increases after the base (first) year's income. For instance, a single lender might offer two participation programs, one taking 5% of each year's gross income and the other program taking 30% of any income above that achieved (or projected to be achieved) in the base year.

As an incentive to the borrower, the face rate of the loan is usually very favorable. Through the participation, however, the lender expects to realize a greater effective interest rate than is obtainable with a conventional loan and additionally may expect a somewhat greater return on the upside alternative due to the additional risk involved in achieving higher income levels. Also, because the lender's yield is greatly enhanced as time passes (assuming the participation amount steadily grows), the lender may require that the loan be locked in (no prepayment) for a stipulated period or that any payoff of the loan be subject to an excessive prepayment penalty.

The obvious disadvantage to the borrower is the reduction in cash flow. Also, the property will suffer from limited marketability, and there will be the lender's requirement for annual audited statements. On the other hand, the borrower's tax shelter position will be enhanced because of the deduction of the participation from reportable income. In times of tight money, the participation loan with its equity kicker to the lender is actually one of the least painful ways for a borrower to obtain financing.

THE CONVERTIBLE MORTGAGE

A convertible mortgage is perhaps the ultimate participation tool in that it gives the lender the option to *convert* its loan into an ownership interest in the property at some predetermined time in the future, perhaps seven to twelve years from the funding date. In turn, the lender grants favorable loan terms and possibly, because the debt service is lower, a larger loan (assuming the loan is underwritten according to a minimum debt-coverage ratio). The conversion option is usually for a percentage of the ownership rather than its entirety.* The property should provide a sufficiently healthy cash flow and/or tax shelter prior to the conversion date if the investor is to realize an adequate return. This type of arrangement initially may appear to favor the lender lopsidedly. However, note that the lender relinquishes its loan when it is converted into the ownership.

This concept can be illustrated more clearly through an example. Suppose that an investor is planning to build an apartment complex and is shopping for the permanent loan. ABC Life Insurance Company offers our investor two deals: Loan A is a 75% of value, conventional 30-year loan at 13.5% interest with monthly payments. Loan B is the same loan but at 12.5% interest and includes an option for the lender to convert its loan to a 55% ownership position at the end of the eighth year. Whichever loan the investor

---

*If the lender does convert to 100% ownership, there is usually an additional cash payment to the borrower.

wants, ABC Life will require a 1.25 debt-coverage ratio. Thus the convertible loan's lower interest rate and payments will enable the lender to make the loan larger than with a conventional loan. Assuming that the first year net income on the new complex will be $120,000, a convertible loan can be made for $750,000* as opposed to a loan of only $706,500 under conventional terms.

The property value on completion is estimated to be $1,000,000, and the most probable projection for appreciation is 6% per year, putting the projected property value at approximately $1,600,000 at option time. If it exercises the conversion option, ABC expects to convert its loan (end of Year 8 balance of $718,598) into an ownership position valued at $880,000 ($1,600,000 × 55%). ABC's increase in wealth is not purely a windfall but includes deferred compensation for the first eight years of favorable interest rates. ABC's true yield is 13.99%. This is 0.49% more than would have been realized with the 13.5% conventional loan and is realistic because of the additional risk involved on ABC's part.

Although the monthly payments are practically identical, the investor benefits by receiving a loan that is $43,500 greater than that obtainable under conventional terms. Also, the investor gets full use of the first eight years' tax shelter. The main disadvantage is the loss of ownership interest. In addition, the lender will probably prohibit any secondary financing, causing the property to suffer from limited marketability prior to the option date. The owner may incur a capital gain tax on conversion, although no cash will be generated for its payment. To circumvent this situation, the borrower may want to require a provision in the loan documents that the lender will fund the amount of such a tax through a loan secured by the borrower's remaining ownership share.

The convertible mortgage is not appropriate for every occasion, but it can be an attractive alternative if money is so tight that lenders require at least some form of participation.

JOINT VENTURES

In the typical real estate joint venture, an institutional lender forms a partnership with a developer for the purpose of developing a property. Thus the two necessary ingredients, money and building expertise, are brought together in a usable form. The developer is the managing partner, handling the construction of the project and managing it on completion. The lender is usually the silent partner, contributing the money in accordance with the

*Annual constant for a 12.5% loan = 0.1281. Maximum loan = $120,100/(0.1281 × 1.25) = $750,039. Round to $750,000.

disbursement schedule or the joint venture agreement. The joint venture agreement also includes the ownership structure, distribution of profits and losses, description of the project, sharing of cost overruns, contingencies, and so forth. Other documents that might be required prior to the signing of the joint venture agreement are the development schedule, development budget, architect's plans and specifications, and the construction contract.

Although the lender will contribute equity money to the project, it may or may not make the construction loan. Many institutional lenders will not make a construction loan under any circumstances because of their lack of expertise in this area. Since higher returns are characteristic of the equity position, the lender may also prefer not to make the permanent loan but may have to as a condition of getting into the deal (the lender may use its stability and financial strength to convince another lender to make the actual loan).

The developer (possibly working through a mortgage broker) initially approaches the lender with possession of the land or an option to purchase it along with an appraisal or feasibility report that supports the profitability of the project. The lender analyzes the project based on criteria that generally include a minimum debt-coverage ratio and an internal rate of return figure. The IRR is based on either a before- or after-tax cash-flow analysis (excluding the developer's portion of the cash flow) that forecasts the return to the lender.

If the lender likes the deal and decides to make the developer an offer, its terms may be very generous. It may contribute 100% of the equity dollars required and even give the developer a development fee during construction and a management fee to manage afterward. Once the property is completed and operating, the lender will probably require an annual preferred return of at least 10% on its equity investment. This return may or may not be cumulative (early year's shortages passed on to following years). After the preferred return to the lender, and depending on the joint venture agreement, the developer may or may not receive a preferred return on its equity. Finally, the remaining cash flow and the reversion upon resale may be split 50–50.

A large part of the lender's decision to go on a particular joint venture rests in the developer's track record. For developers who have the experience, the joint venture route can be very attractive.

MORTGAGE OR DEED OF TRUST?

The contract used for securing the property for the loan's collateral is either a mortgage or deed of trust, although both are often categorized together and called mortgages. The mortgage is used in most states and is a two-party agreement, the parties being the borrower (mortgagor) and the lender (mortgagee). The property is pledged as security and the borrower retains title.

The deed of trust brings in a third party, the trustee, who receives title to the property for security purposes. If the borrower defaults, the trustee can sell the property (without going through court proceedings) and apply the proceeds to the borrower's obligation. The deed of trust is commonly used in the District of Columbia and in about nine states (most notably California). Probably the biggest reason that the deed of trust is not used in other states is that their courts consider a real estate secured loan to be a mortgage, no matter what the form of the instrument is. Hence any default would have to be remedied through court proceedings. There are additional differences between the two documents, including redemption rights, statute of limitations, and deficiency judgments—items that only come into play upon default. Either document should be recorded with the recorder of the county in which the property is situated.

Throughout this book the terms loan, mortgage, and trust deed are often used interchangeably in situations where the actual form of the debt instrument is insignificant.

THE PROMISSORY NOTE

Although the mortgage and deed of trust both act to pledge the property as security for the loan, they seldom contain the actual terms such as amount, interest rate, term, dates, due-on-sale provision, call option, and prepayment penalty. This information is usually contained in a separate document called the promissory note, which contains the promise to pay the loan and the terms of the payment. The note is a negotiable instrument (freely transferable) and is not recorded. The mortgage or deed of trust is actually given to secure the promise of payment that is outlined in the note.

It is possible to have a loan with a note but no mortgage or deed of trust. Upon default, the lender would have only the personal liability of the borrower in seeking satisfaction. On the other hand, it is possible to have a loan without a note, the payment provisions being included in the mortgage or deed of trust. However, most apartment buildings have either a deed of trust or mortgage along with a promissory note.

TO ASSUME OR TAKE SUBJECT TO THE MORTGAGE?

A purchaser taking over an existing mortgage is all too often said to assume the mortgage despite the fact that the purchaser may actually take title subject to the mortgage. When title is transferred and the property is taken subject to the existing loan, the original maker of the note still carries the primary responsibility for repayment. The lender may not even be notified, although it will be receiving the new owner's check. This could only occur technically when there is no enforceable due-on-sale clause to make the balance due and payable upon transfer of title. In times of tight money markets and high interest, many buyers and sellers will often defy the lender's due-on-sale clause, opting for the in-place financing with no origination fees and probably at a lower interest rate. The risk is high, but even if the lender does discover the transaction, there is a good chance that a compromise agreement can be struck between the three parties. The broker negotiating the sale should avoid liability by demanding that the buyer and seller sign an appropriate disclaimer.

This type of transaction typically finds the existing loan at a low loan-to-value ratio, making this a prime situation for a wraparound or second loan. The favorable terms can result in a correspondingly high sale price, necessitating a cash equivalence adjustment before such a transaction can be used as a comparable sale. Cash equivalence is discussed and demonstrated in Chapter 16.

In a true assumption the lender becomes involved and requires a formal agreement that the new purchaser must be primarily liable on the obligation. The lender may also charge an assumption fee, run a credit check, and adjust the interest rate to the current market level.

SECONDS

A second mortgage (or deed of trust) is a loan added on top of a first mortgage. It is created most commonly at the time of purchase or upon a subsequent refinancing of the property during the holding period.

The lender whose repayments are secured by a second mortgage is in a much riskier position than the lender of the first and will usually demand a higher interest rate and a shorter term. The additional risk is due to the subordinated position of the second, whose holder will generally be the one short changed if the borrower cannot afford to make the payments, because claims of the first or senior lender will be satisfied before those of the junior lender. In the case of a default where the property value is no greater than the balance owing on the first, the holder of the second may end up with nothing better than a court-awarded deficiency judgment.

A purchase-money second is a common type of second and is by definition a loan taken back by the seller of the property. This type of loan will often be at an interest rate lower than that available from a lender. In actuality, however, the effective yield is most probably higher because the selling price will be increased accordingly. If the seller doesn't make the second, it will probably be funded by an institutional lender or an individual who buys it through a mortgage broker. When a mortgage broker is used, points charged to the seller as a placement fee are deducted from the loan funding. The broker, possibly a finance company with few assets, can then sell the loan at face value to an investor who finds the high interest rate and short term worth the risk. Rarely is the second considered to be very liquid since commission dollars must be paid if the loan is to be sold again.

WRAPAROUNDS

The wraparound, also known as an all-inclusive trust deed (AITD) is another form of second. The wraparound lender takes over the balance of the first loan (which remains undisturbed), making its payments. The wrap maker also loans new funds, in turn receiving not only payments for the underlying first but also payments on the new money. The borrower pays an enlarged monthly payment to the wrap holder, and the wrap holder in turn pays the underlying first, with the remaining portion of the borrower's payment acting to service the new additional debt.

Wraparounds are used most commonly by sellers who can benefit greatly when the first is at a below market interest rate, although the purchaser may pay close to the market rate for the privilege of obtaining financing. The seller in effect pockets the difference between the interest rate on the first and that charged to the new borrower, thus magnifying the seller's return on the new money loaned. The buyer may benefit from the wraparound interest rate being a point or two below the market level as well as from the absence of origination fees that would ordinarily accompany a new institutional loan. Further, the seller avoids any prepayment penalty. Not limited to transactions, wraparounds can also be arranged during the holding period when an owner needs to pull equity money out through refinancing. In this case, the wraparound loan typically would be arranged through a loan broker, although institutional lenders are slowly moving into this area as well.

Risks on Wraparounds

Wraparounds, subject to some of the risks inherent in any second mortgage, also have some of their own risks. The underlying lender may increase the tax and insurance impound account payments or, if the loan has a variable interest rate, increase the payment. The borrower may be late with a payment, forcing the wrap lender to dig into personal funds to pay the underlying loan. Even more disastrous is the underlying lender choosing to exercise a due-on-sale clause. Although the buyer may eventually pay off a standard second and retain the underlying loan, doing so with a wraparound may require a special clause in the note or prepayment permission from the lender.

Although the interest rate to the borrower is clean cut, the wraparound's true yield to the lender is more difficult to grasp, especially as the underlying loan becomes a larger portion of the total wrap and the interest rate spread increases. The computation of the lender's yield is a must in this type of financing and is covered in the next chapter. Also presented is a method for computing the required wraparound payment and interest rate given the lender's required return.

REFINANCING

Equity growth through appreciation and loan amortization has given apartment building owners a nice piggy bank from which to borrow while still holding on to the property. This opportunity is often taken advantage of, especially when the reinvested money offers a yield greater than the interest rate at which it is borrowed. Possible benefits of pulling out cash through refinancing include:

1. No income or capital gains tax is paid on the borrowed money.
2. The refinanced property shows a decrease in taxable income because of the additional interest deduction.
3. Property marketability may be improved because of the increased loan-to-value ratio.
4. Tax-deferred exchanges become more feasible when equities are balanced through the addition of debt to one of the properties. Not only is the need for cash reduced, but recognized gain can also be avoided.
5. Reinvested proceeds can again be leveraged in another property, magnifying the yield created by appreciation and additional tax shelter.
6. Capital gain can be decreased if a property is refinanced and then subsequently sold through an installment sale.

Refinancing is usually facilitated by an increase in the existing loan or by the addition of a second. The financial feasibility of refinancing can be studied through discounted cash-flow analysis.

LAND CONTRACTS

A land contract is not unique to land sales and can be used to sell and finance apartment buildings or other real estate investments. The most notable characteristic of the land contract is that the seller holds legal title after the sale, at least until the loan is paid off or some other previously agreed on event happens, at which point title is finally passed to the buyer. In the meantime, the purchaser gets possession of the property just as in an ordinary sale. An immediate benefit is that the seller can usually foreclose easier than through a mortgage or trust deed where title has already transferred. Also, without the title passing, the deal is more easily transacted, and the purchaser can buy with less cash and credit because the previous financing usually remains intact.

However, when it comes down to it, the very fact that title does not pass is the reason that the land contract hasn't become popular with apartment building investors. It is not necessary to record a land contract, and the seller may be opposed to doing so, and require a clause in the contract prohibiting recording so that the title won't be clouded and foreclosure can proceed much quicker in the event of the purchaser's default. The purchaser would usually prefer the land contract to be recorded to prevent any subsequent claims on the title and to assure conveyance of title more readily once the contract conditions are met. An additional problem is that financing or refinancing based on a land contract is very difficult.

It would appear that land contracts should be the basis of many creatively financed apartment house transactions. However, the problems involved result in very few buildings changing hands using this instrument. The land contract most likely would be used when the property is substandard, the purchaser has little cash, and third-party financing is an impossibility. If the land contract is used, a competent attorney should be engaged to take care of the legal questions likely to surface prior to the conveyance of title.

CONSTRUCTION FINANCING

Building an apartment complex is almost always financed by means of a construction loan. The construction loan is short term in that it will be due and payable upon completion of the project, at which time the permanent loan will be funded. There are substantial differences between the construction and permanent loans, and most often they are not even made by the same lender.

Construction financing is a specialized field in itself. The loan is funded in increments depending on a disbursement schedule that could specify a monthly draw based on completion or disbursements at various stages of development. Even if the developer has a proven track record, there are many attending risks such as increases in construction costs, delays due to weather, labor strikes, unavailability of materials, environmental legislation, and building code changes. Because of this, interest rates are usually higher on construction loans than on permanent mortgages. The interest rate is not always fixed but may "float" with the prime interest rate during the course of the loan. Hence the rate quoted by the lender may be "prime plus two" for a loan at 2% over the prime, or "prime plus three," and so forth.

Before making a commitment, the construction lender probably will require a previous commitment from a permanent lender to ensure that the construction loan can be paid off upon project completion. On the other hand, the permanent lender may not want to fund until the building reaches a certain income or occupancy level. A typical solution to this problem is a standby commitment in which a third lender promises to make a short-term interim loan between the time of construction loan payoff and the time at which the property meets the funding requirements for the permanent loan. Actually, the standby lender generally hopes that funding won't be necessary so that it can walk off with its commitment fee (probably 1% to 2% of the loan commitment) without ever having paid out a cent. A standby loan doesn't necessarily require an in-place commitment for the permanent loan and can provide the developer with strategies and tactics for obtaining better loan terms because of less risk and possibly lower interest rates at the time the project is completed.

Construction financing involves intricacies that are beyond the scope of this book, and the neophyte developer would do best to seek additional information from a bank, savings and loan institution, mortgage banker, or other entity skilled in this complex field.

POINTS

A loan point is a lump sum cost that the lender charges to the borrower, usually payable upon loan funding. One loan point is the equivalent of 1% of the loan amount—two points on a $100,000 loan equals $2,000. By charging points, the lender increases the loan's true yield. It has been a rule of thumb that one loan point should equal a 0.125% reduction in the loan interest rate. However, various factors, including the actual loan life, have a dramatic effect on the true interest rate. For instance, paying two points on a 12.75%, 30-year loan theoretically should boost the effective yield to 13.00%. However, the effective interest rate is 13.90% if the loan is paid off in two years and 13.19% if the loan is paid off in seven years. Even with the loan going the whole 30-year term, the effective rate is 13.03%, still above the 13.00% effective rate suggested by the guideline.

Points usually are considered by the IRS to be prepaid interest requiring any point charge to be spread over the life of the loan. A different treatment is required if the points are considered a loan origination fee. The tax considerations of points are discussed more fully in Chapter 7.

CHAPTER FIFTEEN

LENDER'S YIELD

When the standard fixed-rate loan was the mode, the lender's yield was the same as the face interest rate of the loan (presuming no point charge). Now that there are point charges and debt instruments like the shared appreciation mortgage and the participation loan, the actual yield can be substantially greater than the face interest rate of the loan. To structure the financing of apartment buildings creatively it is necessary to understand the lender's true yield and to know how to compute it.

The lender's yield is the effective interest rate expected by the lender (and is also the borrower's effective interest rate). We say expected because it is often contingent on the length of the loan or some form of future participation whose timing and dollar amounts have been forecast by the lender. Beyond the normal principal and interest payments, some additional factors that can affect the lender's yield are:

Loan points
Income participation
Uneven payments
Prepayment penalties
Underlying payments (wraparounds)

If the loan is not affected by one of these or similar factors, the lender's yield will be the same as the face rate of the loan. If one or more of these is a factor, the lender's yield will differ from the face rate. An example of this is discussed at the end of Chapter 14, where the face rate of the loan is 12.75% although the lender's yield is increased to 13.19% if two points are charged and the loan projected to be paid off in seven years. Because of the variables involved, the lender generally will require a computation of the loan's forecast yield before making the loan. The lender's yield can be computed as an internal rate of return exercise. This computation is time consuming (see Chapter 11) if there is no access to a calculator that has the IRR procedure hard-wired into it. Calculators that do have this feature are Hewlett-Packard's 12C, Texas Instruments' MBA, and Sharp's EL5102. Watch for these to be replaced by new models. This procedure is accomplished with Calculator Procedure 6.

To compute the lender's yield, the following items must be known or forecast.

Cash outflows (actual money loaned)
Cash inflows (payments, points, equity participations)
Timing of the outflows and inflows

Timing is sometimes based on the expected loan life, which can be forecast as being shorter than the contract (maximum) loan life. Cash outflows are the loan fundings. Most often there is only one cash outflow at the outset of the loan. However, the loan also could be funded in stages with additional funding made even after early principal and interest payments.

The lender's yield traditionally is computed from a before-tax standpoint, although the inclusion of tax factors (such as tax on interest payments received) would add an extra degree of refinement to the computation. Here we will stay with the traditional before-tax method since this will be of most help to lenders in comparing and deciding whether the loan structure meets their yield requirements.

Although it simplifies the yield calculation, the financial calculator has an inherent disadvantage of allowing the operator to do the computation with little feel for what the yield actually means. It is strongly suggested that Chapters 10, 11, and 12 be read and understood before any attempt is made to implement the following techniques.

THE STANDARD FIXED-RATE MORTGAGE—NO POINTS

The yield here is always the face rate, no matter what the holding period is in relation to the amortization period.

THE STANDARD FIXED-RATE MORTGAGE WITH POINTS

Charging points is often the lender's favorite approach to increase the loan's true yield. The points effectively decrease the amount of actual loan funding, meaning that the payments received by the lender are based on a loan amount greater than that actually funded. Consider, for example, the $100,000 loan discussed in the Points section of the previous chapter. By charging two points, the lender effectively reduces the actual funding to $98,000, although the borrower still makes payments on the full $100,000 ($1,086.70 monthly payment based on a 12.75% interest rate with a 30-year term). The cash flows and their timing can be illustrated in the following way.

Month	Cash Outflow	Cash Inflow
0	$98,000	
1–360		$1,086.70

When these figures are entered into the calculator and the internal rate of function is activated (Calculator Procedure 6), the loan's true yield (and the effective interest rate to the borrower) comes out at 13.03%, which is 0.28% greater than the 12.75% face rate.

A more popular concept is that a loan's true life is only expected to be seven years, after which it will be paid off because of resale or refinancing. If this actually happens, the yield will be increased because the point charge is spread effectively over a shorter period. At the end of the seventh year (the eighty-fourth payment), the remaining loan balance (determined by Calculator Procedure 2 and figured on a $100,000 loan amount) of $96,743.54 is paid to the lender along with the eighty-fourth (final) monthly payment. The cash flows and their timing now look like this:

Month	Cash Outflow	Cash Inflow
0	$98,000	
1–83		$ 1,086.70
84		$97,830.24*

*Loan balance plus final monthly payment.

Entering this pattern in the calculator reveals a lender's yield of 13.19%, a yield increase over the same loan without the early payoff assumption.

YIELD ON SECONDS

The cash flows of the second mortgage are easily determined, and the actual life usually has more certainty than the standard fixed-rate loan. Again, with all loans, the internal rate of return is synonymous with yield. Also, it is the same process of outlining the timing of the cash flows and entering them into the calculator.

Example 15-1. *Computing yield on a second.*
A seller is thinking of providing a second trust deed and would like to know the yield. The specifics are:

1. Term: 5 years.
2. Amount: $75,000.
3. Payments: $625 monthly (10% interest only, no amortization).
4. Payoff: full $75,000 due at the end of 5 years.

Q. What is the lender's yield on the second?

Month	Cash Outflow	Cash Inflow
0	$75,000	
1–59		$ 625
60		$75,625

A. Internal rate of return by Calculator Procedure 6:
Yield = 10.00%

LENDER'S YIELD ON A WRAPAROUND

Computing yield on the wraparound mortgage is extremely important because of the two loans and interest rates involved. The cash outflow is merely the amount of new money funded (over the underlying loan), whereas the cash inflows are the payments received in excess of what is necessary to pay the underlying loan. The final payment will include any loan balances to be paid off.

Example 15-2. *Computing yield on a wraparound mortgage.*
An apartment building is sold with the seller wrapping the existing mortgage. The pertinent facts of the two mortgages are:

Existing

Payments $3,866.20 per month

Balance $433,849.03

Interest rate	9.75%
Term	5 years expired on a 30 year term

Wraparound

Amount	$600,000 ($166,150.97 of new money)
Payments	$6,637.20 per month
Interest rate	13.00%
Term	Amortized over 30 years, all due and payable at the end of 5 years

Q. What is the yield to the wraparound lender?

The cash outflow, cash inflow, and timing considerations to the lender are:
Outflow: $166,150.97 funded at time zero.

Inflows and timing: $2,771.00 inflow (payment) per month for the first 59 periods ($6,637.20 less $3,866.20 payment on underlying loan). At the sixtieth period, the last monthly payment plus the loan balance will be due. Calculator procedure 4 will give the entire wraparound loan balance as $588,489.68. The balance of the underlying loan will be $407,603.15. Hence after paying off the underlying loan (or letting the borrower assume it), the wraparound lender receives a payoff of $180,886.53.

The cash flows and their timing are set up like this:

Month	Cash Outflow	Cash Inflow
0	$166,150.97	
1–59		$ 2,771.00
60		$183,657.53

A. The lender's yield is found by entering the cash flows into the financial calculator's internal rate of return function (Calculator Procedure 6).
   Lender's yield = 21.03%

LENDER'S YIELD ON THE CONVERTIBLE MORTGAGE

The lender's yield on the convertible is calculated much the same as it is for a standard loan. The new wrinkle is that rather than receiving a loan balance at the end of the loan term, the lender receives a portion of the property value. The following example is based on the same convertible mortgage discussed in the last chapter.

Example 15-3. *Lender's yield on a convertible mortgage.*

A lender wishes to make a $750,000 mortgage with an option to convert the loan balance into a 55% share of the ownership at the end of the eighth year. The property value, currently estimated to be $1,000,000, is assumed to appreciate at 6% per year to a value of approximately $1,600,000 at the time of the conversion option. The loan is to be made at 12.50% with monthly payments and a 30-year amortization (monthly payments are $8,004.44).

Q. Assuming the lender exercises its conversion option, what is the projected yield to the lender?

With a conversion option at 55% of a projected value of $1,600,000, the lender will receive an ownership share valued at $880,000.

Month	Cash Outflow	Cash Inflow
0	$750,000	
1–95		$ 8,004.44
96		$888,004.44

A. The lender's yield on the mortgage is then found by using Calculator Procedure 6.

Lender's yield = 13.99%

JOINT VENTURE WITH LENDER'S FINANCING AND OWNERSHIP

When a lender goes into an ownership position with a joint venture partner and also provides financing, the lender gets two returns: one on the financing and another on the ownership position. The lender ultimately is interested in the overall return on its combined outlays. There are no new procedures for finding the yield—it is again a matter of identifying the timing, outflows, and inflows.

Example 15-4. *Lender's combined yield on loan and equity positions in a joint venture.*

A lender wishes to enter into a joint partnership with a developer for the purpose of constructing and operating an apartment complex. A condition of this agreement is that the lender is to provide the permanent loan at 14% interest. The cash flows and receipts are as follows:

Time (Months)	Cash Outflow	Cash Inflow	Remarks
0	$ 500,000		Initial equity funding to enter venture
6	500,000		Second equity funding
12	100,000		Final equity funding
12	3,000,000		Loan funding upon completion
13–24	35,546		Monthly loan payment received
13–24	7,500		Monthly return on equity investment
25–36	35,546		Monthly loan payment received
25–36	10,000		Monthly return on equity investment
37–48	35,546		Monthly loan payment received
37–48	11,500		Monthly return on equity investment
49–60	35,546		Monthly loan payment received
49–60	13,000		Monthly return on equity investment
61–71	35,546		Monthly loan payment received
61–71	$14,500		Monthly return on equity investment
72	35,546		Monthly loan payment received
72	14,500		Monthly return on equity investment
72	2,100,000		Lender's share of equity reversion
72	2,952,938		Loan balance to lender

Q. What is the lender's overall yield on the combined equity and loan investment?

First, to simplify entering the figures into the calculator, the cash inflows and outflows are combined, and the zero cash-flow months (during development) are identified.

Month	Cash Outflow	Cash Inflow
0	$ 500,000	
1–5	0	
6	500,000	
7–11	0	
12	3,100,000	
13–24		$ 43,046
25–36		45,546
37–48		47,046
49–60		48,546
61–71		50,046
72		5,102,984

A. The combined yield on loan and equity is found by entering the cash flows into the calculator and using Calculator Procedure 6.
    Combined yield to lender = 15.75%

   The combined yield will always fall between the face rate of the loan and the yield on the pure equity position. Here the loan yield is 14.00% and the yield on equity is 18.60%

CHAPTER SIXTEEN

CASH EQUIVALENCE

The potential sale price for the same property may vary over a wide range because of the variety of available purchase financing. If a property is to be used as a comparable sale and has sold for an inflated price because of some form of favorable financing, some adjustment must be made to the price before a fair comparison can be made to the subject property. This brief chapter offers techniques for:

1. Adjusting comparable sales for favorable financing.
2. Adjusting comparable sales for time-related interest rate differences between the comparable and the subject.
3. Calculating the amount of points to be charged by a lender.

ADJUSTING A COMPARABLE SALE

The need for using the first two techniques arises when a comparable is sold with financing that does not conform to the current market's interest rate or financing structure. For instance, a property would probably sell for two different prices depending on which of the two following financing arrangements could be contracted:

Alternative A

Assumable 8.50% loan, seller to provide secondary financing for remaining 85% of sale price at 11% interest only, all due and payable at the end of 10 years.

Alternative B

75% conventional loan at 14% interest per annum, amortized over 30 years, 25% cash down.

With the favorable financing under Alternative A (more leverage and lower interest), the seller could ask more and the purchaser would pay more than with the conventional financing under alternative B. It is necessary to find what amount of value this favorable financing adds before using such a sale as a comparable. Otherwise the units of comparison (gross rent multiplier, overall rate, and the physical methods) may indicate an artificially high value, reflecting the benefit of financing not necessarily available to the subject property.

The cash equivalence technique provides a method of reducing a comparable's sale price to compensate for favorable financing terms. The comparable sale is repriced with currently available interest rates. The source for typical rates most likely would be an institutional lender or other third party loaning money to the general public at the going rate. Adjusting comparables to market financing is considered the same as adjusting to a cash basis, because a market-rate loan theoretically could be sold for cash to a financial institution or other loan purchaser without any discount off the face value of the loan. Therefore, a loan at the current market rate is already at its cash equivalence and no adjustment need be made.

In essence, the cash equivalence technique might tell us that the comparable that sold for $1,000,000 with favorable financing might have sold for only $925,000 if the owner hadn't carried back low interest rate financing and the first was obtained from an institutional lender at current market terms.

DISCOUNTING THE FACE VALUE OF A LOAN

There will often be a market for a loan—somebody out there will be willing to buy it from a lender (here, a seller who provides financing) for cash. These people constitute the loan purchase market, "make" the rate, and often can be found in the yellow pages and in the financial or classified sections of newspapers. If the loan is purchased at full face value and the same payments are received, the loan purchaser only receives the same rate as the original lender, probably much lower than the loan purchaser requires. The loan payments can't be increased since there is already a contractual agreement. The only way to effectively increase the interest rate is to buy the loan for less than face value. The purchaser (an investor or a loan broker) may purchase a $50,000 owner-carried second for $40,000, thereby increasing the effective interest rate to more than the stated contract rate. In this case, the loan has been sold for a 20% discount ($50,000 − 20% = $40,000). The $40,000 is the cash equivalence of the $50,000 favorable financing. If this loan is used as a comparable, $10,000 would be subtracted first from sale price since it is considered that the property purchaser paid the seller an extra $10,000 to provide the favorable financing. This puts the comparable and subject on equal ground, assuming that the subject is to be offered with typical financing terms (an assumption implicit in the definition of market value). The gross rent multiplier, overall rate, and physical approaches to value can now be abstracted and applied to the subject property. Caution should be used with this method to ensure that the discount rate used isn't so high that only a small percentage of seller/financiers would consider selling the loan at the discount rate.

ANOTHER METHOD FOR COMPUTING CASH EQUIVALENCE

The quickest way to obtain cash equivalence is to discount the face value of the loan in the manner demonstrated above. An alternate technique, actually favored by many as more indicative of market behavior, is to apply the market *interest rate* to the loan income stream, discounting the income stream to a present value or cash equivalent. To adjust a comparable sale:

1. Determine the payments on the loan to be converted, adding any balloon payment to the final periodic payment.
2. Determine today's market rate of interest for such a loan.
3. Using the market rate, discount the income stream (Calculator Procedure 7 for the periodic payment, Calculator Procedure 4 for any balloon payment) to a present value. This is the loan's cash equivalent.
4. Deduct the cash equivalent from the face value of the loan. The remainder is the additional amount paid by the purchaser to obtain the favorable financing.
5. Deduct the additional amount from the comparable's sale price, thereby bringing the comparable and subject to a cash equivalent basis.

This process is demonstrated in the following example.

Example 16-1.   *Discounting a loan to a cash equivalent.*
Research uncovers an otherwise excellent comparable sale that was sold with a favorable second loan. Particulars of the transaction are as follows:

Sale price	$580,000
Cash down	$112,000

First financing	$348,000 (new conventional loan from an institutional lender at the market rate of 14% per annum, amortized over 30 years. Payments are $4,123.36 per month)
Second financing	$120,000 (owner-carried second at 10% interest per annum, payable monthly, interest only, all due in five years. Payments are $1,000.00 per month)
Income	$92,880 annual gross income $60,372 annual net income
Physical description	68 rooms

Q. What is the cash equivalence of the second loan if the market interest rate for similar seconds is 16%?

A. The income stream for the second loan is 59 payments (4 years, 11 months) of $1,000 plus a final payment of $121,000 (final periodic payment plus the payoff). Using Calculator Procedure 7 to discount the series of 59 payments and Calculator Procedure 4 to discount the final payment to a present value gives us the loan's cash equivalence:

Calculator Procedure	Discount Rate	Amount/Type	Present Value
7	16%/12	$1,000 for 59 periods	$40,670
4	16%/12	$121,00 at sixtieth period	54,657
Cash equivalence of second loan			$95,327

Q. What is the sale's cash equivalence for comparable purposes?

A. Adjusting the sale price to a cash equivalence for comparable purposes is done in this way:

Face amount of second	$120,000
Cash equivalence	(95,327)
Price paid for favorable financing	$ 24,673
Sale price	$580,000
Price paid for favorable financing	(24,673)
Cash equivalence of sale	$555,327

Q. What is the indicated gross rent multiplier? Overall rate? Dollars per room?

A. Units of comparison are based on the cash equivalent price:

$$\text{Gross rent multiplier} \quad \frac{\$555,327}{\$\ 92,880} = 6.0$$

$$\text{Overall rate} \quad \frac{\$\ 60,372}{\$555,327} = 10.9\%$$

$$\text{Dollars per room} \quad \frac{\$555,327}{68} = \$8,167$$

Looking at the problem from a different standpoint, the cash equivalent sale price can also be computed as the cash equivalence of the loan plus the cash down payment.

cash equivalent sale price = loan cash equivalency + cash down payment

In Example 16-1 the second question also could have been computed in this way:

Cash equivalence of first	$348,000
Cash equivalence of second	95,327
Down payment	112,000
Cash equivalence of sale	$555,327

SELECTING A RATE

The best method for selecting the appropriate interest rate is to go to the market. In the absence of a market rate for a particular type of loan, a rate must be selected based on other rates, although some adjustment is often needed to reflect the considerations behind the particular loan in question. For instance, the rate for an institutional first would not be applied to a subordinated second that is secured by a higher stratum of the property's value. The following factors are to be considered when selecting the proper market interest rate.

1. *Risk.* Loans are subject to several different types of risk:
   a. Risk of default, especially if the loan is a form of secondary financing and is subordinate to the first.
   b. Risk of no resale market for the loan.
   c. Risk of purchasing power loss.

2. *Liquidity.* By making the loan (or buying it from another lender), the purchaser forfeits the right of immediate access to the funds. Only a periodic loan payment will be realized.

3. *Management.* Management considerations of a loan are usually minimal unless persuasive efforts become necessary to make the borrower pay as agreed. Hence there is also some risk as to the amount of management involved.

The loan interest rate is composed of all three of these factors plus a basic return for the use of the money. An often-used benchmark for composing a market rate is an institutional conventional loan rate adjusted for the risk, liquidity, and management considerations. The benchmark loan and the loan under analysis should be secured similarly, that is, real property, real property plus personal property, and so forth.

Another example of adjusting a comparable sale to its cash equivalent can be taken from the sample valuation report in Chapter 19.

Example 16-2. *Adjusting a comparable sale to a cash equivalent.*
Comparable 3 sold with first and second loans that both reflected favorable financing. Had this comparable not been adjusted to a cash equivalent, its value indicators for the subject would have been very obviously out of line. A summary of the actual rates and terms of the sale are compared to the rates and terms typically available as of the date of valuation:

>   *First Loan*
>   Actual rate: 11.00%   Market rate: 13.75%
>   Actual monthly payments: $4,952

>   *Second Loan*
>   Actual rate: 10.00%   Market rate: 16.00%
>   Actual monthly payments: $1,558

The second loan is for a term of five years, at the end of which the entire balance is due and payable. The investment holding period is based partially on this fact and is projected to be five years. Upon resale of the property at the end of the five years, the first loan will have a remaining balance of $472,790, and the second, payable interest only, will have the entire face amount of $187,000 due.

Q. What is the comparable's cash equivalent sale price?

A. *First Loan Cash Equivalent*

> 59 payments of $4,952 discounted at 13.75% (Calculator $211,513
> Procedure 7)

Sixtieth payment of $477,742* discounted at 13.75%
(Calculator Procedure 4)   241,165
    Cash equivalence of first $452,678

B. *Second Loan Cash Equivalent*

59 payments of $1,558 discounted at 16.00% (Calculator
Procedure 7) $ 63,364

Sixtieth payment of $188,558 discounted at 16.00%
(Calculator Procedure 4)   85,174
    Cash equivalence of second $148,538

Cash equivalent of first $452,678
Cash equivalent of second   148,538

Cash down payment   246,782

Adjusted sale price $847,998

The gross rent multiplier, overall rate, and dollars per unit are now abstracted based on the adjusted sale price of $847,998.

COMPUTING LENDER'S POINT CHARGE

Lenders cannot always afford to lend money at the face interest rate and will often charge points (each point being 1% of the loan amount, usually payable upon loan funding) to increase the effective interest rate (also referred to as the lender's yield). The method for computing the point charge is another type of cash equivalence exercise with several additional steps to the equation. It looks like this:

$$\frac{\text{Face value} - \text{cash equivalence value}}{\text{Face value}} \times 100 = \text{point charge}$$

The cash equivalent value is again figured on the market or required rate.

Although the loan may be based on a 25- or 30-year amortization, this does not necessarily mean that the loan will have a life that long. The lender may retain a call option for a shorter term or expect an early payoff due to resale, refinancing, and so forth. The loan payments would be discounted

*Includes final payment and loan payoff.

over the expected loan life* with the last payment including any balloon payment.

Example 16-3. *Computing the lender's point charge.*

A lender wants to loan funds at 12.00% per annum interest but, due to its own cost of funds, finds it must receive a yield of at least 12.75%. Although amortized over 30 years, the loans will include a call option for the tenth year, which is expected to be exercised. Payments are monthly.

Q. What amount of points must be charged on a 12.00%, $100,000 loan with these terms to bring the lender's yield to 12.75%?

A. The payments for this loan are $1,028.62 per month. A series of 119 of these payments will be received with the one hundred twentieth (final) payment to include the remaining loan balance of $93,416.43. These payments are discounted at the market rate:

Payments	Discount Rate	Calculator Procedure	Cash Equivalent
$1,028.62 for 119 periods	12.75%	7	$69,287
$94,445.05 at period 120	12.75%	4	26,569
Discounted value of loan			$95,856

The discounted value of the loan can now be plugged into the point-charge equation.

$$\frac{\$100,000 - \$95,856}{\$100,000} \times 100 = 4.14 \text{ points}$$

The point charge will probably be rounded off to 4.25, 4.50, or 5 points.

The borrower will pay an up-front charge of $4,250, $4,500, or $5,000 to obtain the loan (depending on rounding practice). Rounding up will place the effective interest rate (lender's yield) slightly above the required 12.75% target.

*Many lenders use the contract life, regardless of the expected life.

CHAPTER SEVENTEEN

TAX-DEFERRED EXCHANGE

When seasoned practioneers discuss apartment house transactions, it often doesn't take long before mention is made of the tax-deferred exchange. Stories about huge brokerage commissions and otherwise profitable property exchanges can be very exciting. All the hoopla is about the tax deferral break that the government somehow decided to give us if we make property exchanges in accordance with rules set forth in Section 1031 of the Internal Revenue Code (hence the origin of the often-used term, 1031 exchange).

To set up an exchange successfully it is necessary to compute whether the investor will recognize any gain (currently taxable) and, further, to compare the investor's position both before and after the exchange to see if the benefits of tax deferral are overshadowed by too reduced a cash flow or equity position. The extent of the required computations may look frightening at first glance but can be made easier by analyzing the concepts involved. The time spent in learning the 1031 exchange techniques should be well recompensated by the profits received on the very first exchange.

WHY A TAX-DEFERRED EXCHANGE?

The outright sale of an apartment building or other real property investment can cause a substantial part of the investor's equity to be lost through the tax on capital gain (assuming the sale price is greater than the adjusted basis of the property). However, by deferring the tax on gain, this usually substantial amount can be reinvested to maximize the investor's wealth. The tax is not avoided; it is only deferred to a future date when the investor disposes of the new property. For instance, a potential capital gain tax of $20,000 deferred for 5 years and invested in the interim at an annual growth rate of 15% would result in a future total of $40,227, leaving the investor with an additional $20,227 after finally paying the IRS its due. By effecting a series of exchanges, one can defer the tax indefinitely.

Other possible benefits that can accompany a 1031 exchange are:

1. Placement of a high basis for depreciation on a property with a lesser market value when trading down.
2. Deferral of recapture of excess depreciation.
3. A higher after-tax cash flow from the new property.
4. Certain deals can be made more easily in a tight money market.
5. Greater expertise can be used to outwit the other party and to end up with a better deal.
6. Pyramiding wealth through upward exchange.

On the other hand, the 1031 exchange is not without its drawbacks:

1. Any capital loss must also be deferred.
2. The depreciable basis for the new property may be lower.
3. A sizable amount of cash may have to be paid to the other party to balance the equities.
4. The new property may have disadvantageous financing.
5. There may be some unleveraging of the equity position.
6. There may be a drop in cash flow.

The exchange should provide benefits that outweigh the drawbacks. Achieving the proper balance for each party requires a degree of expertise. Although the 1031 techniques are not difficult to master, a surprisingly few number of salespeople and investors have sat down to learn them, and this magnifies the value of the expertise of those who have.

PROPERTIES MUST BE "LIKE-KIND"

To effect an exchange with complete tax deferral, the properties exchanged must be "like-kind." The original property must have been held for trade or business purposes and so must the property to be received. A fee interest in any type of real estate traded for another fee interest in a piece of real estate generally qualifies as like-kind tax deferral treatment under Section

1031. Any personal property involved in the exchange (stocks, bonds, cash, promissory notes, etc.) is not considered like-kind property, and the fair market value of the personal property received may be subject to capital gains tax in the year of exchange.

TERMINOLOGY

Certain terminology should be reviewed before proceeding.

Adjusted Basis.   Original basis adjusted up for subsequent capital improvements and down for depreciation.

Boot.   Assets not qualifying as like-kind such as cash, notes, fair market value of personal property, and obligations to render services to make up the difference between unbalanced equities. A purchase-money mortgage on a property conveyed is also considered boot.

Like-Kind Property.   Property with a character or nature similar to another property. Does not refer to class or quality. The main distinction made here is between personal and real property. For instance, vacant land, an apartment building, and an office building would be considered like-kind property.

Net Debt Relief.   The excess of the mortgage traded off over the mortgage on the property received. Net debt relief is considered boot. There can be no negative net debt relief—a party assuming a larger mortgage than that of the transferred property has no net debt relief.

Realized Gain.   Excess of fair market value of property received over the adjusted basis of the property transferred. Any transaction cost would be added to the adjusted basis of the property conveyed, thereby reducing the amount of realized gain.

Recognized Gain.   The taxable portion of the gain. This amount depends largely on the amount of boot received.

MECHANICS OF THE EXCHANGE

Given certain facts about the properties involved, only basic math skills and the ability to follow a simple format are required to make a conclusive analysis:

1. Gather the necessary facts on both the property to be transferred and the property to be received.
2. Balance the equities.
3. Compute the realized gain and net boot received, then choose the lowest figure as the amount of recognized gain from the transaction.
4. Compute the new basis.
5. Analyze the results of the exchange (investor's new equity position, new cash flow, tax deferral, etc.).

EXCHANGE CASE STUDY

This case study analyzes several exchange proposals contemplated by Investor A who is the owner of a 10-unit apartment building.

Required Facts

The following list itemizes the facts that must be obtained to analyze the exchange.

Investor A—Property Profile

Fair market value	$300,000
Mortgage balance	$160,000
Adjusted basis	$145,000
Net income	$ 27,600
Annual after-tax cash flow	$ 6,228
Annual mortgage payment	$ 16,654
Remaining term	24 years
Rate	9.25%
Improvement-to-value ratio	60%
Marginal tax rate	44%

A's tax on an outright sale would be figured:

Sale price	$300,000
Less commission	(18,000)
Less adjusted basis	(145,000)
Capital gain	$137,000
% reportable	40%
Marginal tax rate	44%
Tax on capital gain	$ 24,112

Investor A wishes to avoid the capital gain tax payment and therefore asks you to find another apartment building suitable for exchange and to analyze the postexchange position. You will receive a 6% commission from each party if an exchange is consummated. Your conversations with various sales people quickly leads to Investor B, owner of a 15-unit apartment building that is on the market for either an outright sale or a trade. Investor A inspects B's property and is anxious to exchange. The facts about B's property are:

Investor B—Property Profile

Fair market value	$475,000
Mortgage balance	$290,000
Adjusted basis	$240,000
Net income	$ 42,300
Annual after-tax cash flow	$ 9,687
Annual mortage payment	$ 37,726
Remaining term	27 years
Rate	9.75%
Improvement-to-value ratio	80%
Marginal tax rate	46%

After gathering the required facts, perform the mechanics. Then analyze the new positions of both A and B.

Balancing the Equities

The ownership equity positions (market value less mortgage balance) will seldom be equal, and some amount of boot must be paid by the investor with the smaller equity position to balance the transaction. Investor A has only a $140,000 equity position compared to B's $185,000 equity. Hence A will pay B $45,000 cash boot so that a fair trade can be made. In Exhibit 17-1, the boot paid to the other party is the focal point of the calculation.

Exhibit 17-1. Balancing the Equities

Fair market value	$300,000	$475,000
− mortgage	(160,000)	(290,000)
= equity	$140,000	$185,000
Boot paid to other party	45,000	0
= balanced equities	$185,000	$185,000

Realized Gain, Net Boot Received and Recognized Gain

In Exhibit 17-2, realized gain and net boot received are calculated to arrive at the recognized gain, which is always the lesser of the two. The recognized gain is the amount, if any, that the investor reports for tax purposes in the year of trade. The primary object of an exchange is to have as little recognized gain as possible, although rarely will both parties recognize zero gain. More often, one or both parties will have at least some recognized gain.

Basis of Property Received

The basis of A's new property is the adjusted basis of the property transferred, plus any payments made, plus any recognized gain, less any value received (see Exhibit 17-3).

Exhibit 17-2. Recognized Gain

Realized Gain		
	A	B
Fair market value of property received	$475,000	$300,000
− adjusted basis transferred	(145,000)	(240,000)
+ mortgage transferred	160,000	290,000
− mortgage assumed	(290,000)	(45,000)
+ boot received	0	45,000
− boot paid	(45,000)	(0)
= realized gain	$155,000	$235,000

Net Boot Received		
	A	B
Mortgage transferred	$160,000	$290,000
− mortgage assumed	(290,000)	(160,000)
= net mortgage relief (zero minimum)	0	130,000
− boot given	(45,000)	(0)
= recognized mortgage relief (zero minimum)	0	130,00
+ boot received	0	45,000
= net boot received	0	$175,000
Recognized gain (realized gain or net boot received, whichever is lower)	0	$175,00

Exhibit 17-3. Basis of Property Received

	A	B
Adjusted basis of property transferred	$145,000	$240,000
+ commission	18,000	28,500
+ assumed mortgage	290,000	160,000
+ boot given	45,000	0
+ recognized gain	0	175,000
− boot received	(0)	(45,000)
− mortgage transferred	(160,000)	(290,000)
= basis of new property	$338,000	$268,500

The new basis serves the same purpose as the new basis derived from an outright purchase, being similarly apportioned between land and improvements (see Chapter 7) for depreciation purposes and normally adjusted over the holding period until eventual disposition or exchange of the new property.

Analysis of the Exchange

These figures are practically useless until analyzed for benefits and drawbacks to the investor. The benefits must outweigh the drawbacks. The major items to analyze are the cost to effect the exchange, change in equity position, and change in cash flow:

Investor A—Summary of Change

Item	Before Trade	After Trade	Change/Amount
Fair market value	$300,000	$475,000	+ $175,000
Equity	$140,000	$185,000	+ $ 45,000
Loan balance	$160,000	$290,000	+ $130,000
Loan interest rate	9.25%	9.75%	+ 0.50%
Loan-to-value ratio	53%	61%	+ 8%
Basis	$145,000	$338,000	+ $193,000
First year ATCF*	$ 6,228	$ 16,457	+ $ 10,229
Cash to balance equities		$ 45,000	− $ 45,000
Tax on recognized gain		$ 0	$ 0
Deferred gain		$137,000	+ $137,000
Commission paid		$ 18,000	
Tax on outright sale	$ 24,112		

*Methodology for the ATCF computation is found in Chapters 5 to 8.

Investor B—Summary of Change

Item	Before Trade	After Trade	Change/Amount
Fair market value	$475,000	$300,000	− $175,000
Equity	$185,000	$140,000	− $ 45,000
Loan balance	$290,000	$160,000	− $130,000
Loan interest rate	9.75%	9.25%	− 0.50%
Loan-to-value ratio	61%	53%	− 8%
Basis	$240,000	$268,500	+ $ 28,500
First year ATCF	$ 9,687	$ 13,296	+ $ 3,609
Cash to balance equities		$ 45,000	+ $ 45,000
Tax on recognized gain		$ 32,200	− $ 32,200
Deferred gain		$ 31,500	+ $137,000
Commission paid		$ 28,500	
Tax on outright sale	$ 37,996		

Investor A has paid $45,000 cash (plus $18,000 commission) to effect the exchange. When we review the summary of change for A, certain developments are of immediate note:

1. No gain is recognized on the transaction.
2. Investor A pays $45,000 plus a commission of $18,000 to effect the exchange.
3. Equity will increase by $45,000.
4. Market value will increase $175,000. At five years of 5% annual appreciation, the new property will supply $48,000 of additional equity over the smaller property.
5. The annual after-tax cash flow increases by approximately $10,000.
6. The depreciable basis has increased substantially.

However, as the scenario grows brighter, so does it grow darker. Investor A's benefits are greatly at the expense of Investor B, who, if properly counciled, will want to look for a better deal. The search for Investor A's mate resumes.

ADDING A THIRD PARTY TO THE EXCHANGE

Although the previous example served as a simple introduction to the basic exchange concepts, very few 1031 exchanges are actually of the two-party variety—only 1 to 2% of the total transactions effected by many exchange specialists.

More popular is an exchange among three or more parties, one of whom comes in solely as a purchaser with no property to exchange. Assume that you as a broker find Investor C, who currently has no property for exchange but does have $150,000 available as a down payment. C's motivations and investment criteria lead you to believe that C is a prime candidate to purchase A's property. The position of the three investors can be summarized as follows.

Investor A.   Wants to trade up—would like very much to have B's property.

Investor B.   Wants to trade or sell outright. Not interested in trading for A's property, and the downpayment requirement is beyond the means of C.

Investor C.   Has no property to trade but does have $150,000 cash and a desire to buy an apartment building.

A three way transaction can result in all three investors getting exactly what they want. The pattern and sequence for such a transaction begins as in Figure 17-1.

Investor A is satisfied by receiving B's property. However, B needs to dispose of A's property. This is facilitated through C purchasing it.

Now , A has traded up to B's property, B is cashed out, and C owns A's property (Figure 17-2).

Equity balancing can be done in several ways. Investor A would profit

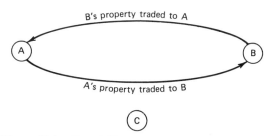

Figure 17-1.   *Step 1.* First part of a three-way exchange.

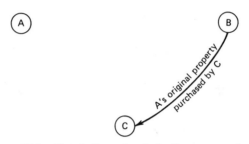

Figure 17-2. *Step 2.* Second part of a three-way exchange.

from additional leverage if a new loan could be placed on B's property prior to the transfer. The exchange contract could be written subject to A's obtaining a new loan on B's property or by B refinancing the property just prior to the transaction. We'll assume that B refinances the property for $335,000 at 12% interest with a 30-year amortization. Informed of the pending transaction, the lender qualifies both Investors A and B to facilitate A's assumption of the loan upon consummation of the transaction.

With the new $335,000 loan, the equities of A and B are now balanced at $140,000 each. There will be no boot involved on the part of either party.

Upon exchanging, Investor B receives A's property with $140,000 in equity and has an additional $45,000 in cash from the refinancing. Combined, this totals $185,000, which is B's equity amount prior to the transaction. Then, as set forth in the three-party exchange agreement, B sells A's property to C, finally pulling out the $185,000 equity in cash.

Investor C has not disposed of any property and, for tax purposes, views the transaction as an outright purchase. However, having disposed of properties, both A and B will be concerned about the tax consequences of capital gain. The recognized gain and new property basis will be the same for both as it would have been with the first proposed transaction.

B will have a recognized gain of $175,000 on the exchange with A. In addition, B will realize a gain on the sale of A's property to C. This will be treated as a long-term gain, because the holding period of the original property is always added to the holding period of the property acquired. The gain on the sale will be as follows.

Exhibit 17-4. Balancing the Equities

Fair market value	$300,000	$475,000
− mortgage	(160,000)	(335,000)
= equity	$140,000	$140,000
Boot paid to other party	0	0

Exhibit 17-5. Recognized Gain

	A	B
Realized Gain		
FMV of property received	$475,000	$300,000
− adjusted basis transferred	(145,000)	(240,000)
+ mortgage transferred	160,000	335,000
− mortgage assumed	(335,000)	(160,000)
+ boot received	0	0
− boot paid	(0)	(0)
= realized gain	$155,000	$235,000

Net Boot Received		
	A	B
Mortgage transferred	$160,000	$335,000
− mortgage assumed	(335,000)	(160,000)
= net mortgage relief (zero minimum)	0	$175,000
− boot given	(0)	(0)
= recognized mortgage relief (zero minimum)	0	175,000
+ boot received	0	0
= net boot received	0	$175,000

Recognized Gain		
Recognized gain (realized gain or net boot received, whichever is lower)	0	$175,000

Exhibit 17-6. Basis of Property Received

Adjusted basis of property transferred	$145,000	$240,000
+ commission	18,000	28,500
+ assumed mortgage	335,000	160,000
+ boot given	0	0
+ recognized gain	0	175,000
− boot received	(0)	(0)
− mortgage transferred	(160,000)	(335,000)
= basis of new property	$338,000	$268,500

Sale price	$300,000
Less commission	(18,000)
Less basis	(268,500)
B's gain on sale	$ 13,500

This will be added to the recognized gain on the exchange and taxed as follows:

Gain on exchange	$175,000
Gain on sale	13,500
Total long-term gain	$188,500

Had B sold the property outright, the gain would have been $206,500. Hence there is $18,000 less gain with the exchange as opposed to a sale, and B saves $3,312 in capital gain taxes on the transaction. This is somewhat deceptive since the $18,000 decrease in gain is due to the commission expense on B's sale of A's property to C. B might not be too pleased about paying two commissions and might require some additional boot or other compensation from A.

The investors' positions are the same as they were under the first proposal, with the following exceptions.

1. A's equity remains unchanged (equities have been balanced previous to the transaction).
2. A's new loan amount is $45,000 greater because of the refinance. The loan-to-value ratio is increased to 71%, and the interest rate is increased to 12%.
3. The first year after-tax cash flow to A is decreased by $2,182 (13% decrease).
4. B cashes out entirely.
5. Investor C enters the picture and now owns A's old apartment building.

Perhaps the most important aspect is that A has deferred the $24,112 tax on capital gain that would have been payable if the property were disposed of in an outright sale.

Although this type of exchange is done frequently, note that the IRS could challenge this format on the step-transaction doctrine in that the two transactions are one, and that the refinancing proceeds received by B is boot received. A safeguard would be to transact the refinance before the exchange transaction is entered into.

QUESTIONS AND ANSWERS

Q. Does vacant land traded for an apartment building qualify as a like-kind property?

A. Yes.

Q. If a single property is exchanged for two properties, how is the basis allocated?

A. The basis is allocated between the properties in proportion to their respective fair market values.

Q. Can a party to an exchange immediately deduct a loss realized on a 1031 exchange?

A. No. Realized losses on exchanges are not deductible, even if boot is received. The loss is reflected in the new basis.

Q. What about brokerage commissions?

A. A paid commission is added to the basis of the new property.

Q. Will a tight money market have an effect on exchanging?

A. Although exchanges are often mentioned as a method of beating a tight money market, they often have disastrous consequences because the equities are more difficult to balance.

Q. Is a valuation of each property necessary to effect an exchange?

A. No. However, it is recommended by some exchange experts and can help keep the exchange stable as more properties and investors are brought into the transaction. Some exchangors also list the values, equities, and loan amounts in the contract.

Q. Does it matter whether an investor taking over a loan assumes it or takes it subject to?

A. No.

Q. How does the IRS treat seller-carried financing in a 1031 exchange?

A. The individual carrying back financing (a "purchase money mortgage") must treat the mortgage as boot received. The boot received is considered to be the fair market value of the note, not necessarily its face value (see Chapter 16 for a thorough discussion on this distinction). An installment sale may be used to spread and defer any gain realized through the carried-back mortgage.

Q. How are furnishings and other personal property treated in a 1031 exchange?

A. Furnishings and personal property are treated like a transfer of cash. The parties involved may wish to transfer the furniture by using a separate contract. Otherwise, the recipient of the furniture would have a realized gain to the extent of the fair market value of the furniture.

CHAPTER EIGHTEEN

INSTALLMENT SALES

Along with the tax-deferred exchange, an installment sale is another type of transaction providing deferral of taxes and capital gain. The gain (and taxes thereon) is spread out over the life of the installment contract (or note) with each year's tax based on the proportionate share of gain received in that year.

At one time the installment sale was of limited use, because only 30% of the sale price could be received by the seller in the year of sale to qualify for such reporting. However, this rule was eliminated by the Installment Sales Revision Act of 1980 (ISRA). Now the seller may elect installment sale reporting if at least one payment is made after the tax year in which the sale took place, regardless of the amount of down payment. For instance, if a property sold in this year, 90% of the sale price could be received at once and 5% received in each of the fourth and fifth years and still qualify for installment sale reporting. Or the sale would qualify if it required nothing down with the total sale price due in five years.

Installment sale rules also apply to seller-carried financing where portions of the sale price are to be received as loan principal over one or more years following the year of sale, even though such financing may not really be intended as an installment sale. The intentional use of the installment sale usually comes when the seller wishes to spread or delay the reportable capital gain over several years in anticipation of a more favorable tax bracket. The drop in tax bracket could result from retirement or a decrease in income. Also, the graduated nature of tax rates favors the recognition of gain over several years rather than in a single lump sum.

PRORATING THE GAIN

The steps in computing each year's gain are:

1. Determine the *amount of gain*.
2. Determine the *amount by which any existing mortgage(s) that will be assumed or taken subject to by the buyer exceed the adjusted basis* (the basis not reflecting any selling expenses).
3. Determine the *contract price* by adding the excess mortgage to the selling price and deducting the full amount of any existing mortgages that the purchaser assumes (or takes subject to). Note that the selling price is not reduced by commissions or other selling expenses paid or incurred by the seller.
4. Determine the percentage of annual principal collections that must be reported as gain ("*gross profit percentage*") by dividing the gain by the contract price.
5. Determine the *amount of principal collected during each year*. Be sure to omit the amount of any interest payments.
6. *Deduct any amount of excess depreciation from the installment payments*. Excess depreciation (discussed in Chapter 7) is recognized as ordinary income and is treated prior to recognition of any capital gain.
7. *Determine the gain reportable in each year* by multiplying the annual principal collections by the gross profit percentage.

This would be the stopping point for tax computation purposes. However, the analysis process requires an additional step:

8. *Analyze the profitability of the installment sale* by measuring the present value of the installments and comparing this to the income as if 100% were received at the time of sale.

Example 18-1. *Computing annual gain reportable on an installment sale.* A seller is contemplating the installment sale of an apartment building. The following are the pertinent facts:

Selling price	$1,000,000
Commission	50,000
Adjusted basis	470,000
Existing mortgage to be assumed by purchaser	650,000
Excess depreciation	0

Seller's receipt of the $350,000 is to be as follows:

Year	Payment
Sale	$100,000
1	0
2	100,000
3	150,000

In addition, the buyer will pay the seller 12% interest on these payments. The reportable gain in each of the four years is outlined in the following steps.

Step 1. Amount of Gain

Sale price	$1,000,000
Commission	(50,000)
Net sale price	$ 950,000
Adjusted basis	(470,000)
Capital gain	$ 480,000

Step 2. Excess Mortgage Over Basis

Existing mortgage	$ 650,000
Adjusted basis	(470,000)
Excess mortgage over basis	$ 180,000

Step 3. Contract Price

Sale price	$1,000,000
Excess mortgage	180,000
Excess mortgage assumed	(650,000)
Contract price	$ 530,000

Step 4. Gross Profit Percentage

$$\text{gross profit percentage} = \frac{\$480,000}{\$530,000} = 90.57\%$$

Step 5.   *Principal Payments*

Year	Principal Payments
Sale	$100,000
1	0
2	100,000
3	150,000

Step 6.   *Excess Depreciation*

(none)

Step 7.   *Gain Reportable*

Year	Principal Payments	Gross Profit Percentage	Gain Reportable
Sale	$100,000	90.57%	$ 90,570
1	0	90.57	0
2	100,000	90.57	90,570
3	150,000	90.57	135,855

INTEREST PAYMENTS—STATED OR UNSTATED

IRS considers each annual payment to include some interest on the indebtedness whether or not this was really the intent of the parties contracting to the transaction. This interest portion of each payment is reported as ordinary income, whereas the remaining principal portion is taxed at the more favorable capital gain rate.

An interest-bearing note carried back by the seller has a stated rate, and the interest portion of the payment is easy to compute (see Chapter 6). The payments often may be entirely interest until the deferred portion of the principle comes due in one lump sum. However, a contract that sets forth only the timing and receipt of the principal payment is said to have unstated interest, and the IRS assigns an interest rate. Or, if the contract stipulates some amount of interest that falls below the IRS testing rate, the payments are then considered by the IRS to carry its imputed interest rate (generally 1% above the testing rate). These rates occasionally change and may be obtained by calling an IRS information number. The phrase commonly used is "testing at 9%, computing at 10%." The seller does best at the lowest interest rate that can be used because of the favorable capital gain treatment on the remaining principal portion, although the purchaser will want a larger portion of the installment sale to be considered interest because of deductibility.

Well-written installment sale contracts usually state the amount of interest due on the principal payments. Where no rate is stated, the interest is computed semiannually on any principal payments due more than six months after the date of sale or exchange. The following steps are necessary in figuring the unstated interest and prorating it over the payments.

1. Using the IRS interest rate on a semiannual basis, compute the present value of any payments to be received six or more months after the transaction date. This is done with Calculator Procedure 7, entering one-half the rate and spacing the consecutive annual payments with one zero each to facilitate the conversion from annual to semiannual.

2. Subtract this amount from the total amount of the payments (not discounted) to obtain the total unstated interest under the contract.

3. A pro rata share of the unstated interest is accorded each payment. This is done by multiplying each payment by a fraction, the numerator of which is the total unstated interest under the contract and the denominator the total of all principal payments due six or more months after the transaction date.

Example 18-2. *Computation and allocation of unstated interest.*

An apartment building is sold through an installment sale but without any interest provision stated in the contract. The contract calls for the buyer to obtain a new loan, pay the seller $100,000 down, and make the following deferred payments.

Number of Months Deferred	Payments
12	0
24	$ 25,000
36	25,000
48	25,000
60	50,000
	$125,000

The IRS imputed interest rate is 10%. The amount and allocation of unstated interest are computed in the following manner.

Step 1.   Present Value of Payments

The payments are discounted to a present value using Calculator Procedure 7 with a 5% rate (semiannual conversion of 10%) and the following cash flow pattern.

Cash Flow Sequence	Payment
0	0
1	0
2	0
3	0
4	$25,000
5	0
6	25,000
7	0
8	25,000
9	0
10	50,000

Present value = $86,840

Step 2.   Total Unstated Interest

Total payments	$125,000
Present value of payments	(86,840)
Total unstated interest	$ 38,160

Step 3.   Allocation

Share of each payment IRS considers interest $= \dfrac{\$38,160}{\$125,000} = 30.5\%$

Months Deferred	Payment	Interest Share	Interest Portion	Principal Portion
12	0	30.5%	0	0
24	$25,000	30.5	$ 7,625	$17,375
36	25,000	30.5	7,625	17,375
48	25,000	30.5	7,625	17,375
60	50,000	30.5	15,250	34,750

Discounting without the use of a financial calculator and more on the application of the test rate can be found in IRS Publication 537, *Installment and Deferred-Payment Sales.*

EXCESS DEPRECIATION

Any amount of excess depreciation taken during the holding period is deducted from the amount of capital gain and taxed at the ordinary rate. It is recognized and taxed before any capital gain portion, being deducted from the principal portion much the same as any unstated interest.

The following example demonstrates the treatment of excess depreciation and serves as the model used in analyzing the feasibility of an installment sale from the seller's viewpoint.

Example 18-3. *Installment sale with excess depreciation.*
An investor sells an apartment building under an installment sale contract with the following particulars.

Sale price	$1,500,000
Commission	75,000
Adjusted basis	475,000
Existing mortgage to be assumed by purchaser	0
Excess depreciation	65,000

The buyer is to obtain a new loan, paying off the $1,050,000 existing loan. The remaining $450,000 is to be paid to the seller in the following installments. The buyer also must pay the seller 12% interest on the outstanding balance (assume 12% is greater than the test rate for unstated interest).

Year	Payments	Interest at 12%
Sale	$100,000	(n/a)
1	0	$42,000
2	0	42,000
3	25,000	42,000
4	25,000	39,000
5	300,000	36,000

The gain reportable for each payment is computed using the following steps.

Step 1.   *Amount of Gain*

Sale price	$1,500,000
Commission	(75,000)
Net sale price	$1,425,000
Adjusted basis	(475,000)
Capital gain	$ 950,000

Step 2.   *Excess Mortgage Over Basis*

(not applicable)

Step 3.   *Contract Price*

Sale price	$1,500,000
Excess mortgage	0
Existing mortgage assumed	(0)
Contract price	$1,500,000

Step 4.   *Gross Profit Percentage*

$$\text{gross profit percentage} = \frac{\$950,000}{\$1,500,000} = 63.33\%$$

Step 5.   *Principal Payments*

Year	Principal Payments
Sale	$100,000
1	0
2	0
3	25,000
4	25,000
5	300,000

Step 6.   *Excess Depreciation*

Down payment	$100,000
Excess depreciation	(65,000)
Remaining principal payment	$ 35,000

The $65,000 excess depreciation will be treated as ordinary income. The remaining $35,000 of the down payment will be treated as gain.

Step 7. Gain Reportable

Year	Principal Payments	Gross Profit Percentage	Gain Reportable
Sale	$ 35,000	63.33%	$ 22,165
1	0	63.33	0
2	0	63.33	0
3	25,000	63.33	15,833
4	25,000	63.33	15,833
5	300,000	63.33	189,990

SELLER'S ANALYSIS OF AN INSTALLMENT SALE

It is often desirable to compare the installment sale to an outright sale with its recognition of all income and tax in the year of sale. The installment sale differs from an outright sale in two ways: the income is realized over a period of time, and, due to the graduated nature of income taxation, the taxes are based on different tax brackets (providing the seller's marginal tax rate is under 50%). The comparative analysis between the two sale methods is done by discounting the installment sale cash flows back to the present and making a direct comparison to the outright sale. The installment sale would be desirable to the extent that its after-tax present value exceeds the after-tax receipts of an outright sale.

TAX RATES

The cash flows from the *operation* of the property are converted to after-tax figures by use of the investor's marginal tax rate (tax rate on top dollar of income). Since installment sale receipts are so large and, for the small investor, may cover several income tax brackets, the investor's tax on other income (wages, stocks, etc.) should be estimated and then deducted from the total tax on other income and installment sale income combined. This procedure calls for the projection of tax rates and investor's other income—two somewhat tenuous figures. The reliability and projection risks of the figures must be considered before one can look at the comparison realistically.

DISCOUNT RATES

The future cash flows are discounted to a single value (described in Chapter 11) at a rate that represents the investor's interim loss of return on the installments. The rate chosen is an after-tax rate that recognizes not only the tax consequence differences in investment vehicles but also the difference between the treatment of the capital gains portion and the ordinary income portion of the installments. The discount rate selected for the following exercise is 16%.

ANALYSIS PROCESS

The analysis process can only commence when each year's gain has been computed. The annual income tax attributable to the installment sale proceeds is determined based on the gain. This is demonstrated in Exhibit 18-1.

Items from the sale that are treated as ordinary income (column 3) are added to the investor's other income (assumed here to be $40,000 at the time of sale and increasing $5,000 annually). Gain reportable is also added but only to the extent that it must be declared as income (40%). The total of these items is shown in Column 5. The tax on the entire income is determined by using the appropriate tax table (column 6). Then the tax on the other income (assuming no sale) is deducted from the total tax, leaving the tax attributable to the sale (column 6).

In Exhibit 18-2, columns 1 and 2 demonstrate the taxes on the sale being deducted from the principal and interest payments received, resulting in column 3, the true after-tax receipts to the investor.

Exhibit 18-3 depicts the discounting of the cash flows back to their present values at the year of sale. The commission has not yet been accounted for and can now be deducted from the present value. The total of the present values less the commission represents the present worth of the installments and will be compared directly to the net reversion from an outright sale—the next amount to be determined. The net reversion computation is covered in Chapter 9, and the details of the mechanics will not be presented here. Note, however, that the tax on capital gain has been figured using the tax tables rather than the investor's marginal tax rate. Exhibit 18-4 computations result in a net reversion of $142,167.

Comparing the proceeds from an outright sale with the present worth of the proceeds from an installment sale results in a $26,391 ($168,558 − $142,167) increase in wealth to the seller choosing the installment method. The analysis has been based on projected income and tax rates and is also influenced

Exhibit 18-1. Tax Attributable to Installment Sale

1	2	3	4	5	6	7	8
Year	Other Income	Excess Depreciation and Interest Income from Sale	40% of Gain Reportable	Total Income Taxable at Ordinary Rate	Tax on Total Income*	Tax on Other Income	Tax Attributable to Sale
Sale	$40,000	$65,000	$ 8,866	$113,866	$ 59,593	$12,657	$46,936
1	45,000	42,000	0	87,000	41,213	15,317	25,896
2	50,000	42,000	0	92,000	44,613	18,067	26,546
3	55,000	42,000	6,333	103,333	52,319	20,817	31,502
4	60,000	39,000	6,333	105,333	53,679	23,943	29,736
5	65,000	36,000	75,996	176,996	103,784	27,093	76,691

*1980 Schedule × tax table.

Exhibit 18-2. After-Tax Receipts

	1	2	3
Year	Principal and Interest Received	Tax Attributable to Sale	After-Tax Receipts
Sale	$100,000	$46,936	$ 53,064
1	42,000	25,896	16,104
2	42,000	26,546	15,454
3	67,000	31,502	35,498
4	64,000	29,736	34,264
5	336,000	76,691	259,309

Exhibit 18-3. After-Tax Installment Sale Proceeds Discounted at 16%

			Years		
Start	1	2	3	4	5
$ 53,064					
13,883	$16,104				
11,485		$15,454			
22,742			$35,498		
18,924				$34,264	
123,460					$259,309
243,558	Present value of installment sale proceeds				
(75,000)	Sales commission				
$168,558	Present value comparative figure				

Exhibit 18-4. Computation of Net Reversion Under an Outright Sale

Sale price	$1,500,000
Commission	(75,000)
Mortgage balance	(1,050,000)
Tax on capital gain	(192,037)
Tax on excess depreciation	(40,796)
Net reversion	$ 142,167

greatly by the selected discount rate. The risks and uncertainties associated with these projections must be considered when deciding which sales technique to use.

Although the 16% discount rate favors the installment sale, it may be desirable to determine at what rate the cash flows could be discounted to equal the benefits from an outright sale precisely—the discount rate at which the seller would be indifferent about which method of sale to use. This is an internal rate of return problem (Calculator Procedure 6) in which the initial outflow is the net reversion under an outright sale, reduced by any immediate receipts due from the installment sale and increased by the amount of commission and sale costs.

Net reversion from outright sale	$142,167
Immediate receipts from installment sale	(53,064)
Commission	75,000
Initial outflow	$164,103

Entering $164,103 into the calculator as the initial outflow and entering the after-tax installment sale proceeds from Years 1 through 5 as the cash flows results in an IRR of 20.2%. If the seller's required discount rate is below 20.2%, the seller will favor the installment method over an outright sale. With a required discount rate of 20.2%, the seller will be indifferent about which sales technique to use. If the seller requires a rate over 20.2%, the outright sale will be favored.

PART FOUR

REPORT WRITING

CHAPTER NINETEEN

REPORT WRITING

Unless the valuation or analysis is kept internal or performed by the actual investor, the findings must be reported to the client and can be done in as little as a phone conversation or as much as a 200-page bound report. Time permitting, professionalism most often demands at least a brief report outlining the findings and their documentation. It must be clean of excess material, yet thorough enough to support a decisive conclusion.

A report is not merely a presentation of the mathematical computations developed, but uses a sufficiently simple narrative description in interpreting these figures and drawing a conclusion. The reader is considered throughout the planning and writing of the report: How much time will the reader have to read it? What terms and procedures must be defined? What photos and graphics will be of help? What topics will be of most interest and concern?

The report should begin with the purpose of the report and should end with the main conclusion or recommendation, followed by the underlying assumptions and limiting conditions of the report and an addendum containing burdensome materials that might otherwise interupt the flow of the report.

This book's first two sections, Valuation and Investment Analysis, draw two different types of conclusions requiring different reports. The valuation report generally is written for a seller, and the analysis report is written for a potential purchaser. The formats are similar, however, and can be identical in some areas of coverage. Outlines for both types of reports followed by actual samples comprise the major portion of this chapter. These outlines and reports are not meant to be ultimate models—each valuation or analysis job presents a unique combination of circumstances, and the client, property, and market will determine what is needed for the particular problem at hand. Bear in mind during the writing of the report that eventually it may be a useful tool in convincing a lender that the property is worthy of a loan.

Special care should be given to the Underlying Assumptions and Limiting Conditions that are found at the end of each of the sample reports. Those cited do not comprise a comprehensive list by any means, and additions should be made as required to protect the valuator or analyst from any malpractice actions. Malpractice insurance should be carried for this type of work.

There should be no hesitation to expand on topics that are out of the usual or that otherwise merit extra consideration, perhaps even giving such a topic its own heading in the report. If the report is abbreviated, that is, if it omits certain computations or comparables, those items should be kept and filed for possible future documentation.

VALUATION REPORT OUTLINE

  I COVER LETTER (bound in report)
- A. Summary of previous contact
- B. Property address
- C. Financing summary
- D. Valuation conclusion
- E. Date
- F. Listing recommendation
- G. Marketing time
- H. Set next communication

  II TITLE PAGE
- A. Title
- B. Photo
- C. Address
- D. Client name
- E. Date
- F. Author
- G. Table of contents

  III PURPOSE
- A. Purpose of report
- B. Interest valued
- C. Property address
- D. Date
- E. Methods used in valuation

IV LOCATION
    A. Street address
    B. Intersections
    C. Proximity to landmarks
V PROPERTY DESCRIPTION
    A. Date of inspection, people present, access to which units
    B. Number of units and unit mix
    C. Quality, style, and type of building
    D. Age, remaining life
    E. Neighborhood
    F. Type of roof
    G. Parking
    H. Current management
    I. Type of tenancy
    J. Occupancy level
    K. Condition
    L. Deferred maintenance, cost to cure
    M. Site size, topography, drainage, zoning regulations
    N. Landscaping
    O. Amenities
    P. Operating expenses—who pays what
    Q. Maintenance contracts
    R. Rent control
    S. Condo conversion possibilities
    T. Conclusion on physical property
VI INCOME AND EXPENSES
    A. Basis and source for estimation
        1. Owner supplied information
        2. Neighborhood rent survey (grid in Addendum)
    B. Relation of rents to current market level
    C. Income and expense statement
        1. Gross income
        2. Vacancy and collection loss
        3. Effective gross income
        4. Expenses
        5. Net operating income
VII FINANCING
    A. Current Loan (include following details if assumable)
        1. Type of loan
        2. Loan balance
        3. Origination date, original term

   4. Lender and loan number
   5. Payment
   6. Interest rate
   7. Remaining term
   8. Whether or not assumable
   9. Prepayment penalty
  B. Most probable structure of sale financing
   1. Type of loan, source
   2. Interest rate
   3. Loan-to-value ratio
   4. Point charges
   5. Additional loans
   6. Cash down payment

VIII COMPARABLE SALES
  A. Matrix of indicators
  B. Reference comparable data in addendum
  C. Discuss indicator selection process
  D. Select most appropriate indicators

IX VALUATION—apply indicators to subject property

X CORRELATION AND FINAL VALUE ESTIMATE
  A. Summarize valuation results
  B. Comment on appropriateness of approaches used
  C. Comment on reliability of information
  D. Comment on decision process
  E. Valuation date
  F. Interest valued
  G. Final value estimate(s)
  H. Suggested listing price and terms
  I. Marketing time

XI UNDERLYING ASSUMPTIONS AND LIMITING CONDITIONS
  A. Author's relationship to client and interest in property
  B. Reliability of information sources
  C. Financing assumptions
  D. Responsibility for legal and title considerations
  E. Responsibility for physical defects and government regulations
  F. Review of title report, policy, or survey

XII AUTHOR'S SIGNATURE AND DATE

XIII ADDENDUM
  A. Title
  B. Table of contents
  C. Photos

D. Maps
E. Current rent roll
F. Comparable rents
G. Owner-supplied documents
H. Comparable sales
I. Extraneous computations
J. Miscellaneous

Exhibit 19-1

Mr. and Mrs. John Smith
4128 Laredo Drive
Metropolis, CA 99112

Dear Mr. and Mrs. Smith:

In accordance with our meeting on July 9, I have personally inspected and performed a market valuation study for your apartment building located at 213 S. Willson Avenue in Metropolis. The following report summarizes my findings and provides documentation for the estimates of value.

The market value of the property is contingent partially on whether you provide any financing yourselves. A small majority of sellers currently are carrying back second mortgages at below market interest rates, realizing some increase in sale price.

As of July 16, 1982, based on conventional financing only, my findings support a market value of from $630,000 to $650,000. A most reasonable listing price would be $665,000. Secondary financing of $25,000 at 10% interest, all due in 5 years, would increase the value and suggested listing price by approximately $5,000. Assuming proper marketing, a reasonable sale time would be from one week to 60 days.

I will be contacting you in the next few days to discuss the marketing of this property. In the meantime, don't hesitate to call me with any questions regarding this report.

Sincerely,

William Jones
Real Estate Broker

SAMPLE VALUATION REPORT

Valuation Report

For the property located at:

213 S. Willson Avenue
Metropolis, California

Property value as of July 16, 1982

For: Mr. and Mrs. John Smith

By: Mr. William Jones

Contents

Item	Page
Purpose	X
Location	X
Property description	X
Income and expenses	X
Income and expense statement	X
Financing	X
Valuation	X
Correlation and final value estimate	X
Underlying assumptions and limiting conditions	X
Addendum	X

Purpose

The purpose of this report is to estimate fair market value of the fee ownership for the subject property as of July 16, 1982. Fair market value is defined as

> The highest price in terms of money which a property will bring in a competitive and open market under all conditions requisite to a fair sale, the buyer and seller, each acting prudently, knowledgeably and assuming the price is not affected by undue stimulation.

Real Estate Appraisal Terminology
Byrl N. Boyce, Editor

The valuation methods used in the following study are those recognized as most accurately reflecting current market behavior of apartment building sellers and purchasers.

Location

The property is located in the City of Metropolis on the west side of South Willson Avenue between Lamme and Lyon Avenues. The site is approximately two miles east of the Fashion Square regional shopping center and one mile north of the Interstate 41 Washington Boulevard exit.

Property Description

The subject property was inspected on July 16, 1982, with the on-site manager present. Interior access was made to units 3, 7, 9, and 11 (manager's unit).

The subject property is a 25-unit apartment building containing 15 one-bedroom units and 10 two-bedroom units, all with one bath. The building was constructed in 1972 and has an estimated remaining economic life of 30 years. It is located in a residential area composed of average quality, 1,000 to 1,700 square foot, single-family residences (price range $90,000 to $140,000) with one- and two-story apartment buildings of four to 35 units located along arterial streets. City zoning precludes commercial or industrial use for at least a three-block radius.

The property is currently owner managed with an on-site resident manager who maintains the landscaping, coordinates maintenance work, and shows apartments for rent. The resident manager's fee is $200 per month plus a free one-bedroom apartment. The building is currently 100% occupied under month-to-month rental agreements, mostly by young working singles and childless couples. A survey of the area found only four units vacant of the total 156 surveyed (2.6%).

The property is in good condition with the only deferred maintenance noted being a nonoperative wall air-conditioner in Unit 12. The cost to cure this problem is estimated to be $300.

The building is of wood frame construction with stucco siding and a flat (with drainage slopes), built-up composition roof. Windows are aluminum-framed casement. Each unit has at least two Peerless wall air-conditioners, one dishwasher, disposal, and built-in range and oven. One-bedroom units contain approximately 650 square feet, and two-bedroom units contain approximately 800 square feet.

The site is zoned R-4 and contains 24,327 square feet with 120 feet of frontage along Willson Avenue. A concrete driveway along the south side leads to the rear parking lot with space for 25 cars, each space having a shade canopy. The topography is flat. A concrete block wall belonging to the subject property runs along the side and rear property boundaries. The subject sides northerly to a single-family residence, sides southerly to a 12-unit apartment building, and fronts across Willson to single-family residences.

The landscape is well designed for minimal maintenance and lends an attractive appearance to the building with grassy areas and numerous shrubs and deciduous trees. A built-in sprinkler system covers approximately 75% of the landscaped areas.

With the exception of cold water and exterior lighting, all utilities are paid for individually by the tenants. All units have a 30-gallon water heater, owner-supplied carpeting, drapes, free-standing General Electric refrigerators, and Peerless stoves. None of the units have any owner-provided furniture.

Income and Expenses

An income and expense statement has been prepared to estimate the annual gross income, expenses, and resulting net income as of the date of this report.

Income figures are based on the property's July 1982 rent roll. A neighborhood rent survey with appropriate adjustments (see Exhibits A-1 and A-2 in the Addendum) supports market rents of $350 for the one-bedroom units and $450 for the two-bedroom units. Most units appear to be rented below the prevailing rates, creating a monthly loss in gross income of $535 (5.5% of the market rent roll). However, no upward adjustment will be given for valuation purposes since the comparable sales are also believed to have had similar below-market rents. Also, note that the manager's unit is accorded market rent in the following statement with the manager's total compensation reflected under expenses. Three percent has been deducted from gross income to account for vacancy and collection losses. Expense figures are predicated partially on the owner-supplied 1980–1981 Operating Statement, which can be found in the Addendum as Exhibit B.

Income

4 (1-1) @ $290	$1,160
9 (1-1) @ $340	3,060
2 (1-1) @ $350	700
7 (2-1) @ $425	2,975
3 (2-1) @ $440	1,320
	$9,215
	× 12

Annual gross income	$110,580	
Less vacancy and collection loss @ 3%	(3,317)	
Effective gross annual income		$107,263

Expenses

Fixed		
Property taxes	$14,300	
Insurance	1,400	
Variable		
Electric	340	
Water	750	
Repairs, maintenance, and decorating	5,200	
Refuse	680	
Resident manager's salary	2,400	
Resident manager's apartment	4,200	
Miscellaneous	300	
Reserves		
Carpeting (25 @ $575/5 years)	2,875	
Drapes (25 @ $100/5 years)	500	
Refrigerators (25 @ $420/10 years)	1,050	
Stoves (25 @ $330/10 years)	825	
Wall air-conditioner (60 @ $300/10 years)	1,800	
Total expenses	(34.1%)	(36,620)
Net operating income		$ 70,643

Financing

The property currently is encumbered with a 8.50% interest rate loan with Metropolitan Federal Savings & Loan (Loan No. 6-834776). The loan was originated in 1972 in the amount of $350,000 and currently has a balance of $314,117 with 20 years and one month remaining before the loan completely amortizes. Monthly payments are $2,672.27.

In a telephone discussion on July 13, 1982, Mr. Albert Weiss, Loan Officer for Metropolitan, said that the company would automatically activate the due-on-sale clause upon any transfer of ownership (without prepayment penalty). Since the loan cannot be assumed, anyone purchasing the property would have to obtain new financing. Financing for this property most probably would be from a local savings and loan association. Mr. Weiss said that Metropolitan would consider making a new conventional loan at 13.75% interest for 75% of the appraised value, to be amortized over 30 years. One point would be charged up front. A survey of five other savings and loans and three mortgage brokers indicates that Metropolitan has the most attractive financing package.

In the current market, approximately two-thirds of the conventionally financed sales have owners carrying back second mortgages for some additional portion of value, usually at rates from 10% to 13% per annum with full payoff at the fifth anniversary. Inclusion of this type of secondary financing may have some impact on sale price and is addressed further in the Reconciliation and Final Value Estimate section of this report.

Research uncovered four recent comparable sales and one current listing (Comparable 5). Exhibit C in the Addendum summarizes the salient facts of the comparables and Exhibits D-1 through D-5 provide complete details on each one. The following are abstracted value indicators to be used in the various approaches to value.

Valuation Approach	Comparable				
	1	2	3	4	5
Cash flow rate	4.7%	3.0%	5.9%	4.0%	1.7%
Gross rent multiplier	6.1	5.3	5.9	5.5	6.0
Overall rate	11.0%	12.2%	10.9%	11.9%	10.9%
Adjusted dollars per unit	$26,750	$23,558	$25,925	$24,439	$26,232

Based on analysis of the subject property and the corresponding attributes of the comparables, a single value indicator for each approach is selected as being most appropriate for the subject property. The selection process considers the physical attributes of each comparable property, time of sale, financing, buyer and seller motivations, reliability of information, and so forth. The selected indicators are:

Valuation Approach	Selected Indicator
Cash flow rate	4.0%
Gross rent multiplier	5.8
Overall rate	11.0%
Adjusted dollars per unit	$26,000

Valuation

Each of the techniques and their selected indicators are applied to the subject property to obtain the respective value estimates.

Cash-Flow Rate. A cash flow rate of 4.0% has been selected as that currently required by purchasers when buying this type of property. Further, this is based on a 25% equity (cash down payment) position with a 75%-of-value first loan—typical financing in the present market. The current interest rate is 13.75% with a 30-year amortization period. Using the band of investment technique, these parameters will be used in building an overall rate that will be applied to the subject's net income in estimating value.

Band of investment technique

$0.75 \times .1398 = 0.1049$
$0.25 \times .0400 = \underline{0.0100}$
Overall rate $= \overline{0.1149}$

$$\text{value estimate} = \frac{\text{net income}}{\text{overall rate}} = \frac{\$70,643}{0.1149} = \$614,822$$

Round to $615,000

Gross Rent Multiplier (GRM). A gross rent multiplier of 5.8 is deemed appropriate for the subject property.

value estimate $=$ GRM $\times$ gross income $= 5.8 \times \$110,580$
value estimate $= \$641,364$
   Round to: $640,000

Overall Rate. Rather than building an overall rate, as was done in the first approach, the rate is abstracted directly from the comparables. The selected overall rate is 11.0%.

$$\text{value estimate} = \frac{\text{net income}}{\text{overall rate}} = \frac{\$70,643}{0.110} = \$642,209$$

Round to: $640,000

Adjusted Dollars per Unit. In this approach, each comparable's purchase price is divided by its number of units to arrive at a dollar-per-unit sale price. Since the subject and comparables each have different earning capacities per unit, an income-per-unit ratio is computed for the subject and each comparable with this ratio then applied to the comparable's dollar-per-unit sale price. The result is the adjusted dollars per unit. The adjusted dollar per unit figure most applicable to the subject is $26,000.

value estimate $=$ number of units $\times$ dollars per unit
value estimate $= 25 \times \$26,000 = \$650,000$

Correlation and Final Value Estimate

The four approaches provide a value range from $615,000 to $650,000:

Cash flow rate	$615,000
Gross rent multiplier	$640,000
Overall rate	$640,000
Adjusted dollars per unit	$650,000

The reliability of the information used in each approach is considered satisfactory. However, the information for each comparable was collected from outside sources, a factor that favors the reliability of gross income figures over net income since it has a more standard definition and is less prone to computation error. The numerical order of the comparables is felt to be representative of their similarity to the subject property in terms of physical improvement, tenancy, management, time, and terms of sale.

In the current market, great emphasis has been placed on cash-flow rates and gross rent multipliers. Secondary emphasis is placed on the overall rate approach. The adjusted dollars per unit seems to be more of a psychological barrier for most buyers, who are not willing to go above $30,000 per unit.

The identical value estimates produced by the GRM and OAR approaches build a strong case for a property value of $640,000. However, a sale at this price would provide the purchaser with only a 2.2% cash-flow rate as opposed to the 4.0% rate considered more appropriate to this market. Only Comparable 5, an unsold listing, has a cash-flow rate of 2.2% or lower.

With a conventional loan at market rates and terms for 75% of sales price and a 25% cash down payment, it is my opinion that the value of this property ranges from $630,000 to $650,000. A reasonable listing price, subject to negotiation, would be $665,000.

It is current policy for local lending institutions to allow second mortgages behind their new firsts as long as the property can maintain a break-even, before-tax cash flow. A 13.75%, 30-year loan for 75% of a $650,000 sale price and the subject indicated net income of $70,643 would allow a 10%, interest only second loan for five years in the amount of approximately $25,000 to be placed on the property. If the seller were to carry back such a loan, it is my further opinion that market value and listing price could be enhanced by an additional $5,000.

Based on my findings as documented in the report, it is my opinion as of July 16, 1982, that the market values and reasonable listing prices of the fee interest for the subject property are:

Financing	Value Range	Suggested Listing Price
75% of value conventional loan at market rates and terms, 25% cash down.	$630,000–$650,000	$665,000
75% loan, $25,000 owner-carried second at 10% interest for five years, remainder to be cash down payment.	$635,000–$655,000	$670,000

Assuming proper marketing, sale time would be from one week to 60 days.

Underlying Assumptions and Limiting Conditions

This Valuation Report is subject to the following underlying assumptions and limiting conditions.

   1. The author of this report declares that he has a current interest in the property in the form of a possible sales commission.

   2. The information in this report furnished by others is believed to be reliable, but no responsibility for its accuracy is assumed.

   3. No responsibility is assumed for matters involving legal or title considerations.

   4. No opinion is intended to be expressed on matters that require legal expertise or specialized investigation or knowledge beyond that customarily employed by real estate sales people.

   5. No responsibility is assumed for hidden defects or conformity to specific governmental requirements such as those for fire, building and safety, earthquakes, or occupancy codes.

_____   _____

Date   William Jones
                                                                Real Estate Broker

Addendum

213 South Willson Avenue
Metropolis

Item	Exhibit
Rent comparables	A-1 through A-2
1980–1981 operating statement	B
Summary of comparable sales	C
Sales comparables	D-1 through D-5

Exhibit A-1. Adjustments for Deriving Market Rental of One-Bedroom Apartments

Item	Subject	145 S. Willson	238 S. Willson	400 S. Willson
Rent		$335	$340	$355
Condition	Good	Average +$10	Good —	Average +$10
Parking	1 covered per unit	1 covered per unit —	1 open per unit +$5	1 covered per unit —
Stove/Refrigerator	Yes/Yes	Yes/Yes —	No/No +$15	Yes/Yes —
Pool	No	No —	Yes −$5	No —
Furnishings provided	No	No —	No —	Yes −$20
Total adjustments		+$10	+$15	−$10
Adjusted rent		$345	$355	$345

Based on these adjusted rent comparables, the indicated market rent for the subject property one-bedroom units is:

$350

Exhibit A-2. Adjustments for Deriving Market Rental of Two-Bedroom Units

Item	Subject	310 N. Willson	145 N. Willson	238 S. Willson
Rent		$450	$440	$435
Condition	Good	Good —	Average +$10	Good —

Item	Subject	310 N. Willson	145 N. Willson	238 S. Willson
Parking	1 covered per unit	1 open per unit + $5	1 covered per unit —	1 open per unit + $5
Stove/refrigerator	Yes/Yes	Yes/Yes —	Yes/Yes —	No/No + $15
Pool	No	No —	No —	Yes + $5
Dishwasher	No	Yes − $10	No —	No —
Patio	No	Yes − $10	No —	No —
Total adjustment		− $15	+ $10	+ $15
Adjusted rent		$435	$450	$450

Based on these adjusted rent comparables, the indicated market rent for the subject property two-bedroom units is:

$450

Exhibit B.   1980 and 1981 Operating Statement*

213 South Willson Avenue Metropolis		
Income	1980	1981
Rental units	$78,671	$86,223
Expenses		
Utilities	690	842
Gardening	800	—
Resident manager	1,500	2,400
Painting	550	538
Insurance	1,114	1,114

Exhibit B. *(Continued)*

213 South Willson Avenue
Metropolis

	1980	1981
Expenses		
Plumbing repairs	790	540
Electrical repairs	325	—
Real estate taxes	12,768	13,350
Depreciation	9,330	9,330
Interest payments	28,805	28,421
Miscellaneous	3,958	5,730
Total expenses	$60,630	$62,265
Net income	$18,041	$23,958

*This document is supplied by owner.

Exhibit C.   Summary of Comparable Sales

	1	2	3	4	5
Sale price	$500,000	$560,000	$847,998*	$415,000	$560,000
% cash down	30%	15%	32%	20%	25%
Date	3-12-82	12-5-81	2-1-82	6-14-82	Current
Number of units	20	29	35	18	19
Proforma					
Gross income	$ 82,400	$105,400	$144,900	$ 74,950	$ 93,900
Expenses	27,192	37,100	52,164	25,500	32,865
Net operating income	55,208	68,300	92,736	49,450	61,035
Annual debt service	48,108	65,816	78,124	46,147	58,722
Before-tax cash flow	$ 7,100	$ 2,484	$ 14,612	$ 3,303	$ 2,313
Indicators					
Cash-flow rate	4.7%	3.0%	5.9%	4.0%	1.7%
Gross rent multiplier	6.1	5.3	5.9	5.5	6.0
Overall rate	11.0%	12.2%	10.9%	11.9%	10.9%
$/Unit	$ 25,000	$ 19,310	$ 24,229	$ 23,056	$ 29,474
Adjusted $/Unit	$ 26,750	$ 23,558	$ 25,925	$ 24,439	$ 26,232

*Comparable Sale 3 sold for $935,000 with favorable financing. The cash equivalent sale price is $848,702 based on market interest rates. GRM, OAR and Adjusted $/Unit indicators are based on $848,702 cash equivalent selling price.

Exhibit D-1. Sale Comparable 1

[Picture]

Address: 2120 N. Gates Avenue, Metropolis

Distance from subject property: 2 miles N.W., near Juanita St.

Sale price: $500,000　　　Date: 3-12-82　　　Cash down: $150,000 (30%)

Financing: 70% first at 13.5% interest, 30 years. Investor's First Bank. 30% cash down.

Cash-flow rate: 4.7%　　Gross rent multiplier: 6.1　　Adjusted $/unit: $26,750
　　　　　　　　　　　Overall rate: 11.0%

Property description: 20-unit, one story center court built in 1975. Average quality, good condition. Some location detriment due to lack of street parking. Otherwise, neighborhood is similar. 20 on-site parking spaces. All units include refrigerator, wall air-conditioner. No pool.

Gross Rent: $82,400　　Expenses: $27,192 (33%)　　Not operating income: $55,208
Annual debt service: $48,108　　　Before-tax cash flow: $7,100
Comments: Best comparable for subject property. Was on market for 19 days.

Information source: Multiple Listing Service, County Assessor

Exhibit D-2. Sale Comparable 2

[Picture]

Address: 570 S. Grand Avenue, Metropolis

Distance from subject property: 1½ miles west, near Fashion Plaza Shopping Center

Sale price: $560,000　　　Date: 12-5-81　　　Cash down: $84,000 (15%)

Financing: 70% first at 14.00%, 30 years (Savings and Loan)
　　　　　15% second at 12.00% interest only, all due in 10 years

Cash-flow rate: 3.0%　　Gross rent multiplier: 5.3
　　　　　　　　　　　Overall rate: 12.2%　　Adjusted $/unit $23,558

211

Exhibit D-2. *(Continued)*

Property description: 29-unit, 2-story, side walk-up built in 1970. Above average quality. Average condition. Slightly superior neighborhood. Heated pool.

Gross rent: $105,400   Expenses: $37,100 (35%)   Net operating income: 68,300

Annual debt service: $65,816   Before-tax cash flow: $2,484

Comments: Good leverage with only 15% down. Was on market 3 days.

Information source: Appraiser

Exhibit D-3. Sale Comparable 3

[Picture]

Address: 8532 E. Niles Street, Metropolis

Distance from subject property: ½ mile north, near Fairview and Culbertson

Sale price: $935,000*   Date: 2-1-82   Cash down: $246,782 (26%)

Financing: Assumable first at 11.00% with remaining balance of $501,218 (54%), 24 years remaining on 30-year loan.
Annual payment = $59,424.
Owner-carried second for 20% of sale price at 10% interest, payable monthly interest only, all due in interest, payable monthly interest only, all due in 5 years. Payments = $1,558 per month.

Cash-flow rate: 5.9%   Gross rent multiplier: 5.9*
                    Overall rate: 10.9%*   Adjusted $/unit $24,229*

Property description: 35-unit, two-building, side walk-up built in 1975. Average quality. Average condition. Similar neighborhood. All units are furnished. Tenants are somewhat more transient. Pool.

Gross rent: $144,900   Expenses: $52,164 (36%)   Net operating income: $92,736

Annual debt service: $78,124   Before-tax cash flow: $14,162

Comments: Listing broker says rents were 15% below market. Was on market for 23 days.

Information source: Multiple Listing Service, listing broker

---

*Due to favorable financing, sale price of $935,000 has been converted to cash equivalent of $847,998 on which gross rent multiplier, overall rate and adjusted $/Unit are based. Calculated on 5-year holding period with 13.75% market rate for first loan, 16% market rate for second loan.

212

Exhibit D-4. Sale Comparable 4

[Picture]

Address: 8051 Rasmussen Street, Metropolis

Distance from subject property: $\frac{3}{4}$ mile west, near Reserve Street

Sale price: $415,000   Date: 6-14-82   Cash down: $83,000 (20%)

Financing: 80% seller wraparound with 13.50% effective rate, 22 years remaining

Cash-flow rate: 4.0%   Gross rent multiplier: 5.5   Adjusted $/unit $21,442
Overall rate: 11.9%

Property description: 18-unit, two-story, side walk-up built 1980. Above average quality. Good condition. Slightly better neighborhood. Good location for shopping. Lot is bottle-shaped with 50-foot frontage, 80-foot rear lot line—minimum adverse effect. No pool. No furnishings or appliances. Does have wall air-conditioner. Flood hazard area.

Gross rent: $74,950   Expenses: $25,500 (34%)   Net operating income: $49,450

Annual debt service: $46,147   Before-tax cash flow: $3,303

Comments. Expense figures not available—$25,000 is an estimate. Was on market for 55 days.

Information source: listing broker, County Assessor

Exhibit D-5. Sale Comparable 5

[Picture]

Address: 10251 Bishop St., near City Drive

Distance from subject property: 2 miles west, near Horner and Third

List price: $560,000   Date: current   Cash down: $140,000 (25%)

Financing: Buyer to obtain new first. Owner will not carry any financing—needs cash.

Cash-flow rate: 1.7%   Gross rent multiplier: 6.0   Adjusted $/unit 23,284
Overall rate: 10.9%

Exhibit D-5. *(Continued)*

Property description: 18-unit, one-story, center court built 1967. Average quality, average condition. Slightly inferior neighborhood. Tenants are less stable than in subject property. No pool. Central air-conditioner with utility cost paid by landlord.

Gross rent: $93,900   Expenses: $32,865 (35%)   Net operating income: $61,035

Annual debt service: $58,722   Before-tax cash flow: $2,313

Comments: *This comparable is a listing*—on market for 32 days. Rents at about market. Broker says no serious bites.

Information source: listing broker, MLS

ANALYSIS REPORT OUTLINE

    I   COVER LETTER (bound in report)
        A.   Summary of previous contact
        B.   Reference the written report, also submitted
        C.   Brief property description
        D.   Offering price, terms, and cash investment
        E.   Summary of analysis report
        F.   Conclusion and recommendations
        G.   Date of next communication
   II   TITLE PAGE
        A.   Title
        B.   Photo
        C.   Address
        D.   Client name
        E.   Date
        F.   Author
        G.   Table of contents
  III   PURPOSE
        A.   Purpose of report
        B.   Property address
        C.   Date
        D.   Analysis and valuation methods used
        E.   Basis of assumptions
  IV   ASSUMPTIONS
        A.   Purchase price
        B.   Cash down, closing costs

    C. Financing
    D. Income
    E. Expenses
    F. Depreciation
    G. Holding period
    H. Resale amount
    I. Investor's marginal tax rate
    J. Management strategy

V LOCATION
    A. Street address
    B. Intersections
    C. Proximity to landmarks

VI PROPERTY DESCRIPTION
    A. Date of inspection, people present, access to which units
    B. Number of units and unit mix
    C. Quality, style, and type of building
    D. Age, remaining life
    E. Neighborhood
    F. Type of roof
    G. Parking
    H. Current management
    I. Type of tenancy
    J. Occupancy level
    K. Condition
    L. Deferred maintenance, cost to cure
    M. Site size, topography, drainage, zoning regulations
    N. Landscaping
    O. Amenities
    P. Operating expenses—who pays what
    Q. Maintenance contracts
    R. Conclusion on physical property

VII COMPETITION AND DEMAND
    A. Other units in area—existing and under construction
    B. Vacancy rates
    C. Subject's competitive advantages and disadvantages

VIII PROPOSED FINANCING
    A. Current financing—assumable or not
    B. Proposed financing
        1. Structure of financing
        2. Type of loan and source
        3. Amount and percent of price

         4. Rate
         5. Term
         6. Points
         7. Prepayment penalty
         8. Assumable on resale
         9. Other provisions
        10. Conclusion

IX PRO FORMA
    A. Basis and source for estimation
        1. Owner-supplied information
        2. Neighborhood rent survey (grid in Addendum)
    B. Relation of rents to current market level
    C. Income and expense statement
        1. Gross income
        2. Vacancy and collection loss
        3. Effective gross income
        4. Expenses
        5. Net operating income

IX VALUATION
    A. Approaches used
    B. Comparables
    C. Value conclusion
    D. Relation to purchase price

X ANALYSIS
    A. Techniques to be used
    B. Assumptions
    C. After-tax cash flow projection
    D. Net reversion
    E. Rate of return
    F. Other return or value techniques

XI CONCLUSION AND RECOMMENDATIONS
    A. Return
    B. Present value and relation to purchase price
    C. Cash flow
    D. Risk and recommendations for outside opinions
    E. Liquidity
    F. Management
    G. Relation to investor's objectives
    H. Purchase recommendation

XII UNDERLYING ASSUMPTIONS AND LIMITING CONDITIONS
    A. Analyst's personal interest

    B. Report based on assumptions—return not guaranteed
    C. Reliability of information
    D. Review of title report, policy, or survey
    E. Expertise limitation
    F. Governmental regulations
    G. Others

XIII ADDENDUM
    A. Title
    B. Table of contents
    C. Photos
    D. Maps
    E. Current rent roll
    F. Owner-supplied documents
    G. Comparable sales and rents
    H. Extraneous computations
    I. Miscellaneous

Exhibit 19-2. Cover Letter

Mr. and Mrs. John Smith
4128 Laredo Drive
Metropolis, CA 99112

Dear Mr. and Mrs. Smith:

The following report is a purchase analysis for the 150-unit apartment building located at 2284 Fifth Avenue in Metropolis. This building has not been made available to the general public but is being offered for sale through an associate of mine to accommodate a tax-deferred exchange.

Although this report estimates the property's value at $6,050,000, I believe it can be purchased for $5,800,000 with $1,800,000 cash down payment (31.0% of purchase price) plus closing costs of approximately $45,000. The financing is very advantageous with an assumable, 10.5% interest first mortgage for 59.2% of the purchase price and a five-year, 12%, owner-carrier second mortgage for 9.7% of purchase price.

Based on certain assumptions outlined at the beginning of the report, the annual rate of return over a five-year holding period is 24.8%. This is an excellent return in comparison to other properties currently being sold. In addition, the property requires practically no owner management and incorporates relatively little risk—characteristics that meet your investment objectives.

Exhibit 19-2. *(Continued)*

This is an unusually good investment opportunity, and I highly recommend that you take advantage of it. I caution you that time is of the essence since the sellers are anxious to complete their exchange. Any consultations with your accountant or attorney should be accomplished immediately. I will call you within the next few days so that we can proceed from here. In the meantime, don't hesitate to call me with any questions regarding the property or report.

Sincerely,

William Jones
Real Estate Broker

SAMPLE ANALYSIS REPORT

Analysis Report

For the property located at:

2284 Fifth Avenue
Metropolis

For: Mr. and Mrs. John Smith

By: Mr. William Jones

Date: August 24, 1982

Contents

Topic	Page
Purpose of this report	X
Analysis assumptions	X
Location	X
Property description	X
Competition and demand	X
Pro forma	X
Valuation	X
Analysis	X
Conclusions	X
Underlying assumptions and limiting conditions	X
Addendum	X

Purpose of this Report

The purpose of this report is to analyze the property located at 2284 Fifth Avenue in Metropolis for a possible purchase by Mr. and Mrs. John Smith. It is currently being offered for sale to accommodate a Section 1031 property exchange being effected by Mr. and Mrs. Robert Johnson and Mr. Steven Berg. In this report, the property is analyzed as an outright purchase using standard valuation and discounted cash-flow analysis techniques.

Analysis Assumptions

The analysis of this report is based on projected cash flows over a five-year holding period. The cash flow projections are based on the following assumptions.

Purchase price	$5,800,000
Cash down	$1,800,000 (31.0%) ± $45,000 closing costs.
Financing	Assume existing first mortgage from Metropolis Firemen's Pension Fund. Balance on 8-1-82 of $3,435,414 (59.2% of purchase price), Monthly payments are $32,245, interest at 10.5 per annum, amortized over 30 years (due 5-1-08), no call option, no prepayment penalty. Two more principal and interest payments before closing transaction.
	Seller to carry back second mortgage for $564,586 (9.7% of purchase price—the difference between current loan balance on first mortgage and $4,000,000). Monthly payments of $5,646 are interest only at 12% per annum with the principal due and payable at the end of the fifth year.
Income	Effective gross income (total income less vacancy allowance) of $695,825 at beginning of first year, increasing 10% per year.
Expenses	Annual expenses without taxes of $148,769 at beginning of first year, increasing 10% per year. Real estate taxes of $75,050 at beginning of first year, increasing 2% per year.
Depreciation	ACRS method over a 15-year life. Improvements represent 70% of purchase price. Depreciation factors based on a beginning-of-year purchase.

Holding period	Five years
Tax rate	Investor has a 50% marginal tax rate.
Resale amount	$9,850,000 (fifth year net income capitalized at 8.1%, the same overall rate that the property is assumed to be purchased at). This represents an annual appreciation rate of 11.2%. Sale costs are 7% of sales price.

Location

The property is located at 2284 Fifth Avenue in Metropolis, approximately 500 feet southwest of the intersection of Sixth Avenue and Kramer Boulevard, approximately one-half mile west of Metropolitan Stadium. Exhibit B in the Addendum of this report is a Location Map.

Property Description

The property was inspected by me on August 22, 1982. No interior inspections were made of any of the units, although a purchase would be contingent on the inspection of a reasonable number of units. Photos of the property comprise Exhibit A in the Addendum.

The property is a 150-unit, two-story garden apartment complex built in 1974. There are 25 buildings, each containing six units. The unit mix is as follows:

Unit Type	Number
1 bedroom/1 bath	102
2 bedrooms/1 bath	48
	150

The buildings are all of similar architecture, having on-grade slab foundations, wood-frame construction, stucco-coated exteriors, and flat ($\frac{1}{4}$ inch per foot drainage pitch) roofs. Liberal use is made of wood and brick trim. Construction quality is slightly above average for apartments built during the same period. Exterior condition is average.

Electricity is separately metered to the individual tenants. Water and gas (cooking, hot water, and laundry room) are master metered.

Although no inspection of the interiors was made, the listing broker told me during an August 21 phone conversation that the unit interiors are in average condition and are well designed with individual gas forced-air heating units, wall air-conditioners, built-in range/oven units, and dishwashers. There are no landlord-provided furnishings other than carpeting and drapes. The units are said to be spacious and attractive. An inspection of at least five of the units is recommended prior to any purchase.

The property was originally well landscaped, although the current management has not given adequate care to the grounds. Trimming is needed on the maple, honey locust, and yellow wood trees, and the beds of juniper shrubs and chamomile ground cover also need attention. All of the 75 lower floor units have small private patios with grapestake redwood fences. Approximately 10 of these fences need replacement of some redwood stakes due to breakage. My estimate for refurbishing these is $2,500. The concrete walkways are in good condition, and approximately 80% of the landscaped area is serviced with built-in sprinklers controlled by electric timers. The property is well lighted, and the lights are controlled by timers. Landscape maintenance expenditures appear sufficient for reasonable care; I would recommend a possible change of landscape maintenance contractors upon purchase of the property.

The buildings are surrounded on the sides and rear by the tenant parking area. There are a total of 225 spaces (1.5/unit), all covered. Carport construction is of 4″ × 4″ wood posts with mineral cap sheet over plywood roofs. Each space has a concrete tire barrier to protect the concrete block walls from bumper damage. The carports and their walls effectively serve to wall the complex from the surrounding properties. The parking and driveway areas are asphalt and are slightly sloped to drains. The six trash container areas are of poured concrete and are well shielded from view. Two laundry rooms are equiped with an adequate number of leased machines providing an annual income of approximately $600.

The site itself is a level, rectangularly shaped parcel with 375 feet of frontage along Fifth Avenue and is 685 feet deep (256,875 square feet or 5.90 acres). It is not in a flood hazard zone and site drainage appears adequate. It is zoned by the City as MDR (Medium Density Residential), which allows a maximum of one dwelling unit per each 1,700 square feet of space (the subject contains one unit for each 1,712.5 square feet). The site sides northerly to a neighborhood of single-family residences ($125,000 to $160,000 price range) and sides southerly to a seven-store neighborhood shopping center. Across Fifth Avenue is Belevedere Public Park, which is attractively landscaped and contains picnic facilities and a branch of the Metropolis City Library. The subject property and the surrounding area constitute a neighborhood of harmonious uses. There are no noted adverse effects.

The property is managed by MM, Inc., a well-known Metropolis apartment management firm. Their fee is 5% of the collected income plus a fee for tax preparation services averaging $300. On-site management is conducted by Mr. and Mrs. Ray Zikalis (Unit 1) and Assistant Manager Barbara Lenoco (Unit 57). The current management appears to be doing an adequate job. Tenants are compatible with a smooth operation and are reliable for rent payments. Tenant occupancy has averaged 1.8 years for the past four years.

In summary, the property is in average condition, is well located, and operates in an efficient manner.

Competition and Demand

An occupancy survey was made by me on August 22, 1982 of 10 similar apartment buildings within a 2-mile radius of the subject. Of the 1,320 units, 22 were vacant, indicating a vacancy rate of 1.7%. As of the same date the subject property had two vacancies (1.8%).

There are currently no known apartment buildings being developed in this area, and demand is expected to continue at the existing level. It should be noted that the City of Metropolis is currently not allowing any condominium conversions due to the lack of available rental units.

Pro Forma

The following income and expenses were provided by the listing broker and are represented as being prepared on 8-1-82 by MM, Inc. and representing the past 12 months. The figures appear reasonable. The debt service charges are as outlined earlier in this report.

Income

Unit rental $386/unit/month average with two units vacant)	$695,210
Laundry room income	615
Total income	$695,825

Expenses

Real estate taxes	$75,050
Electricity	4,125
Gas	12,413
Water	4,129
Landscape	8,500
Insurance	5,813
Professional management	34,406
On-site management	18,750
Rubbish	4,200

Repairs, maintenance, and decoration	34,690	
Carpet replacements	14,900	
Miscellaneous	6,843	
Total expenses	(223,819)	(32.2%)
Net operating income	$472,006	
Debt service:		
First	(386,940)	
Second	(67,750)	
Before-tax cash flow	$ 17,316	

Valuation

On analyzing five sales of similar apartment buildings (more fully covered in Exhibit C in the Addendum of this report), the following indications of property value are considered reasonably accurate.

Valuation Method	Numbers	Value Indication (r)
Gross rent multiplier	8.7 × $695,825	$6,055,000
Overall rate	$\dfrac{\$472,006}{0.080}$	5,900,000
Cash-flow rate*	$\dfrac{\$472,006}{0.078}$	6,050,000
Adjusted dollars per unit	150 × $40,500	6,075,000
Final reconciled value		6,050,000

*The cash-flow rate approach is based on proposed financing, a value of $5,800,000, and a 0% cash-flow rate.

The final purchase price of $5,800,000 represents 96% of the actual market value as estimated in this report.

Analysis

To analyze the investment, conventional cash-flow analysis techniques are used on after-tax cash flows that have been projected over a five-year holding period. The projection assumptions are listed on pages 1 and 2 of this report, and more detailed cash flow projection computations can be found as Exhibit D in the Addendum. Cash flows are assumed to be realized at the end of the respective years. The after-tax cash flow projection over the five-year holding period is:

After-tax cash flow

	Year 1	Year 2	Year 3	Year 4	Year 5
Gross income	$765,408	$841,948	$926,143	$1,018,757	$1,120,633
Expenses	163,646	180,010	198,012	217,813	239,594
Real estate taxes	76,551	78,082	79,644	81,237	82,861
Net income	$525,211	$583,856	$648,487	$ 719,707	$ 798,178
Debt service	454,692	454,692	454,692	454,692	454,692
Before-tax cash flow	70,519	$129,614	$193,795	$ 265,015	$ 343,486
Tax savings	160,462	88,997	34,668		
Tax payable				(23,145)	(84,791)
After-tax cash flow	$230,621	$218,611	$228,463	$ 241,870	$ 258,695

Sale price at the end of the holding period is projected using an 8.1% overall rate—the same that the property is purchased at. Deductions are made for sale costs, loan payoffs, capital gains taxes, and excess depreciation.

Sale price	$9,850,000 (r)
Sale costs (7%)	(689,500)
Loan pay-offs:	
First	(3,256,546)
Second	(564,586)
Gain taxes	(933,767)
Excess depreciation tax	(257,134)
Net reversion	$4,148,467

Rate of Return. A financial management rate of return is used to compute the annual return to the investor based on the $1,845,000 initial investment and the projected cash flows and resale reversion. The rate of return is based on the annual cash flows being invested at 10% until resale at the end of Year 5, at which time the invested cash flows and net reversion proceeds total $5,578,282. Based on these figures, the annual return is:

24.8%

Conclusions

1. Purchase property with terms as set forth in this report. A recommended starting point for negotiations is a purchase price of $5,650,000 with the seller carrying back a second mortgage for 15% of purchase price at 12% interest, principal all due and payable at the end of the fifth year. Loan to be assumable and with no prepayment penalty.

2. After purchase, upgrade landscape improvements as described in the Description of Improvements section of this report.

Underlying Assumptions and Limiting Conditions

1. The author of this report declares that he has a current interest in this property in the form of a possible sales commission.

2. The information in this report furnished by others is believed to be reliable, but no responsibility for its accuracy is assumed.

3. To analyze the property certain assumptions have been made concerning the purchase price, terms, and performance of the property over a five-year holding period. These assumptions are listed on page 1 and 2 of this report.

4. No responsibility is assumed for mathematical errors contained in this report.

5. No responsibility is assumed for matters involving legal or title considerations.

6. No opinion is intended to be expressed on matters that require legal expertise, specialized investigation, or knowledge beyond that customarily employed by real estate sales people.

7. No responsibility is assumed for hidden defects or conformity to specific governmental requirements such as those for fire, building and safety, earthquakes, or occupancy codes.

Date   William Jones
                                            Real Estate Broker

*Addendum**

Item	Exhibit
Subject property photos	A
Location map	B
Sales comparables	C
Extraneous computations	D

*The Analysis Report should include an Adendum consisting of the items listed. It is not included here. The Addendum would be similar to that of the Valuation Report earlier in this chapter.

CALCULATOR PROCEDURES

Several years ago, shortly after advances in electronics finally lead to the proliferation of inexpensive hand-held calculators, various subspecies were developed that were tailored specifically to the needs of professionals involved in such areas as engineering, statistics, chemistry, and finance. These calculators were revolutionary in that they provided instantaneous accessibility to techniques and routines that were previously available only through the use of main-frame computers or cumbersome and laborious mathematical tables and formulas. Financial calculators suddenly made present values, future values, rates of return, loan payments, and loan balances only a few button touches away. Real estate schools and professional organizations have been quick to bring the calculator to their classrooms, greatly enhancing the recognition, credibility, and acceptance of discounted cash-flow techniques such as those found in this book.

There are presently three companies marketing hand-held financial calculators: Hewlett-Packard, Sharp, and Texas Instruments. On the low end of the price range is Texas Instruments' Business Analyst-II. The Business Analyst-II performs all of the calculator procedures outlined in this book with the exception of number 6, the internal rate of return. If the IRR capability is desired, a somewhat more expensive calculator such as Hewlett-Packard's 12C, Sharp's EL-5102, or Texas Instrument's MBA must be used. All of these calculators are available at a variety of stores and come with easy to follow instruction manuals. Depending on the type of calculator and the source, all of these calculators should cost between $45 and $150.

There are seven different financial calculator routines used in solving the more difficult problems contained in this book. The following pages outline the seven procedures and provide step-by-step examples in using the Business Analyst-II and 12C. The Business Analyst-II has been chosen because of its popular price. The 12C is also popular—mainly because of Hewlett-Packard's user support in the form of special real estate and finance applications books. Another benefit of the 12C is that it is also a miniature computer that can be programmed easily with up to 99 steps—a feature whose usefulness becomes more apparent once the few minutes are taken to learn this capability.

Because of the ever-changing advances in electronics, these calculators are sure to be replaced with fancier and more powerful models including personal computers. Some shopping at variety and personal computer stores will uncover what's new. However, the seven routines outlined here will maintain their validity no matter what calculator is used, and cross referencing between the following procedures and the calculator's instruction book will identify the exact procedure for the particular calculator.

CALCULATOR PROCEDURE **1**

LOAN PAYMENT

Required Variables

(a) Loan amount
(b) Number of payments
(c) Interest rate

Example

A borrower needs a $210,000 loan which is to be amortized over 30 years at 11.75% interest per annum with monthly payments. What is the borrower's monthly payment?

BUSINESS ANALYST-II   *Mode: FIN*

Enter		Display	Comments
210000	PV	210000.00	Enters the loan amount.
30	×	30.00	Number of years in the loans times
12	= n	360.00	months per year equals the number of payments during the life of the loan.
11.75	÷	11.75	Annual interest rate divided by
12	=	0.98	the number of payments per year equals the periodic interest rate.
	%i	0.98	Enters 0.098 (actually carried out to eleven decimal places) as the periodic interest rate.
2nd	PMT	2119.76	Answer*

HP12-C

Enter	Display	Comments
210000 [PV]	210,000.00	Enters the loan amount.
30 [g] [n]	360.00	Enters the number of monthly payments over the 30-year period.
11.75 [g] [i]	0.98	Enters the periodic interest rate (display answer is rounded).
[PMT]	−2,119.76	Answer*

*The answer to four decimal places is $2,119.7605. The actual payment will most likely be $2,119.77 since the lender usually rounds up.

NOTE.   These examples assume that the decimal place read-out on each calculator is set at two.

CALCULATOR PROCEDURE 2

LOAN BALANCE

Required Variables

(a) Loan payment
(b) Number of payments from beginning to end of payment period
(c) Interest rate per annum
(d) Number of payments per year
(e) (For BA-II) original amount of loan

Example

A loan was originally made in the amount of $210,000 at 11.75% per annum interest amortized over 30 years. Monthly payments are $2,119.77. What is the remaining loan balance after the end of the first year (12 payments)?

BUSINESS ANALYST-II   Mode: FIN

Enter		Display	Comments
			First, go through the steps of Calculator Procedure 1 to find the loan payment. Round to two decimal places.
2119.77	PMT	2119.77	Enters monthly payment.
2nd	N	359.99	Finds number of payments (final payment will be a portion of $2,119.77.
12	2nd		
	Acc/Bal	24632.58	Displays interest paid.
	x≷y	209195.34	Answer. Remaining loan balance after 12 monthly payments is $209,195.34.

HP-12C

Enter	Display	Comments
2119.77 [CHS] [PMT]	− 2,119.77	Key in the payment, change it to a negative, and enter it.
210000 [PV]	210,000.00	Loan balance at start of calculation.
11.75 [g] [i]	0.98	Annual interest rate converted into a periodic interest rate.
12 [f] [AMORT]	− 24,632.60	Total amount of interest paid during the 12 payments.
[RCL] [PV]	209,195.36	Answer. Remaining loan balance after 12 months is $209,195.36.

NOTE.   Two-cent difference in BA-II and 38C answers is caused by internal rounding.

CALCULATOR PROCEDURE **3**

FINDING THE FUTURE VALUE
OF A KNOWN PRESENT
AMOUNT

Required Variables

(a) Present value
(b) Number of growth periods (usually years) from present to future date
(c) Growth rate

Example

A cash flow of $11,015 is generated by an investment in Year 1 (assumed to be realized at the end of the year). It is invested to yield 8% per annum for the remainder of the five-year holding period. What will its worth (future value) be at the end of Year 5 (four growth periods).

BUSINESS ANALYST-II Mode: FIN

Enter		Display	Comments
11015	PV	11015.00	Enters the present value.
8	%i	8.00	Enters 8 as the growth rate.
4	n	4.00	Enters 4 as the number of compounding periods.
2nd	FV	14985.79	Answer. The $11,015 will grow to $14,986 over four years at an 8% per annum growth rate.

HP-12C

Enter		Display	Comments
11015 CHS PV		− 11,015.00	Enters a negative 11,015 as the present value (regarded as a cash *outflow*).
8	i	8.00	Enters 8 as the annual growth rate.
4	n	4.00	Enters 4 as the number of compounding periods.
	FV	14,985.79	Answer. The $11,015 will grow to $14,986 over four years at an 8% growth rate per annum.

CALCULATOR PROCEDURE **4**

FINDING THE PRESENT
VALUE OF A KNOWN
FUTURE AMOUNT

Required Variables
(a) Future value
(b) Number of periods (usually in years) to the future date
(c) Discount rate

Example

A $48,857 renovation project at the end of Year 3 of the holding period
is undertaken. The reinvested Year 1 and Year 2 cash flows plus the
Year 3 cash flow—totaling $2,486—will be applied to these costs,
creating a shortfall of $46,371. What amount must be invested at the
start of the holding period to make up the $46,371 shortfall? Assume a
20% reinvestment rate.

BUSINESS ANALYST-II   Mode: FIN

Enter		Display	Comments
46371	FV	46371.00	Enters 46,371 as the required future amount.
20	%i	20.00	Enters 20 as the interest rate at which the amount will be invested.
3	n	3.00	Enters 3 as the number of compounding periods.
2nd	PV	26835.07	Answer. $26,835 invested at a 20% per annum growth rate will equal $46,371 in three years.

HP-12C

Enter		Display	Comments
46371	FV	46,371.00	Enters 46,371 as the required future amount.
20	i	20.00	Enters 20 as the interest rate at which the amount will be invested.
3	n	3.00	Enters 3 as the number of compounding periods.
	PV	− 26,837.07	Answer. $26,835 invested at 20% per annum will equal $46,371 in three years.

CALCULATOR PROCEDURE **5**

GROWTH RATE (FMRR)

Required Variables

(a) Initial cash outlay
(b) Total reversion at the end of the holding period
(c) Length of holding period (years)

Example

An initial cash outlay of $93,000 has grown to an amount of $201,622 at the end of the five-year holding period. What is the rate of return (FMRR)?

BUSINESS ANALYST-II   Mode: Fin

Enter		Display	Comments
93,000	PV	93000.00	Enters initial cash outlay.
5	N	5.00	Enters years in holding period.
201622	FV	201622.00	Enters the reversion (includes reinvested cash flows).
2nd	%i	16.74	Answer. The annual rate of return is 16.74%.

HP-12C

Enter		Display	Comments
201622	ENTER	201,622.00	Enters total reversion.
93000	÷	2.17	Divides by the initial outlay to find the total growth.
5	f 1/×	0.20	Enters the number of years in the holding period and finds its reciprocal.

HP-12C   *(Continued)*

Enter		Display	Comments
$\boxed{g}$	$\boxed{y\times}$	1.17	Determines annual growth rate.
$\boxed{f}$	4	1.1674	Displays to four decimal places.
1	$\boxed{-}$	0.1674	Answer. The annual rate of return is 16.74%.

CALCULATOR PROCEDURE **6**

INTERNAL RATE OF
RETURN (IRR)

Required Variables

(a) Initial investment
(b) Subsequent cash flows

Example

A seller makes a wraparound mortgage. The amount of money funded
is $166,150.97. The payments to be received are $2,771.00 for 60
months with the final payment including a balloon payment to the seller
of $180,886.53. What is the seller's annual yield (effective interest rate)
on the wraparound?

BUSINESS ANALYST-II

The Business Analyst-II does not have a built-in internal rate of return
capability. The BA-II can only compute an IRR by a trial-and-error
process in which the cash flows are discounted at various rates until the
rate is found that discounts the cash flows to equal the initial investment
precisely. This rate is the IRR.

HP-12C

Enter			Display	Comments
166150.97				
CHS	g	CFo	− 166,150.97	Enters the initial outflow as a negative.
2771	g	CFj	2,771.00	Enters the montly payment receipt.
59	g	nj	59.00	Enters number of payments to be received.
183657.53				
	g	CFj	183,657.53	Enters total of final periodic payment and balloon payment.

HP12-C   (Continued)

Enter			Display	Comments
	f	IRR	1.75	Monthly yield.
12	×		21.03	Answer. The seller's annual yield is 21.03%.

CALCULATOR PROCEDURE **7**

PRESENT VALUE OF A SERIES
OF PAYMENTS

Required Variables

(a) Payments and their timing
(b) Discount rate

Example

A series of 59 monthly payments of $1,000 are to be received. The
annual discount rate for finding the present value equivalent of these
payments is 16%. What is the present value of the payments?

BUSINESS ANALYST-II   Mode: FIN

Enter		Display	Comments
1000	PMT	1000.00	Enters 1,000 as the amount off each monthly payment.
59	N	59.00	Enters the number of payments.
16 ÷ 12 = %i		1.33	Enters the annual discount rate converted to a monthly rate.
2nd PV		40669.99	Answer.

HP-12C

Enter		Display	Comments
1000 CHS PMT		− 1,000.00	Enters a negative 1,000 as the amount of each monthly payment.
59	n	59.00	Enters the number of payments.
16	g i	1.33	Enters the annual discount rate converted to a monthly rate.
PV		40,670.00	Answer.

GLOSSARY

Abstract. To break down economic and/or physical attributes of a comparable property into units of comparison that can be applied to the corresponding attributes of the subject property to arrive at an estimate of value for the subject property.

Adjusted basis. The original basis adjusted for subsequent depreciation (adjustment down) and capital improvements (adjustment up).

After-tax cash flow (ATCF). The amount of annual cash return to the investor after provisions for operating expenses, mortgage payments, federal income tax payments as a result of the investment, and so forth. As presented here, the ATCF does not include the consequences of state income tax.

Annual constant. The total annual loan payments expressed as a percentage of the initial loan amount.

Amortization. Gradual payment of a debt through a series of payments. A portion of the payment customarily is used to pay the periodic interest on the debt with the remaining portion going toward amortizing or decreasing the amount of the debt itself.

Basis. The cost of a property (assuming an outright purchase) that not only includes the purchase price but costs incidental to obtaining the title as well.

Before-tax cash flow (BTCF). The annual cash flow derived by deducting loan payments from net operating income. It does not take into account the income tax consequences of the investment for the investor. Also known as cash flow.

Capitalization. The process of converting an income stream into an estimate of value for the asset providing the income stream.

Cash flow. See Before-tax cash flow.

Cash-flow rate. The before-tax cash flow to the investor after operating expenses and debt service are paid, expressed as a percentage of the initial equity investment. Also known as the cash-on-cash return or the equity dividend rate.

Comparable sale. Another property sale from which comparative units of value are abstracted to apply to the subject property.

Compound. Growth of a single deposit or series with the growth rate continually applied to the immediately previous balance.

Debt service. Loan payments—usually an annual figure.

Depreciation. An accounting concept in which the investor is able to deduct a certain portion of the improvement value each year (for tax purposes) under the theory that the improvements are continuously deteriorating and losing value. This is a big boost to the tax shelter provided by the property because it is not a true out-of-pocket expense.

Discounted cash flow (DCF). A form of investment analysis that measures the performance of an investment based on cash flows projected for the expected holding period.

Discounting. The act of discounting cash flows receivable in the future back to the present, thereby accounting for the time preference of money. The reciprocal process of compounding.

Discount rate. The rate at which cash flows are discounted back to the present. The discount rate should reflect the rate of return available from a competitive investment opportunity with some possible adjustment for differences in risk, liquidity, and management.

Disposition. The sale or exchange of a property.

Effective gross income (EGI). The potential gross income less an allowance for vacancy and collection losses.

EOY (end of year). By convention, projected cash flows in real estate investment analysis are assumed to be realized at the end of the year.

Equity. The investor's monetary interest in a property measured as the difference between total value and the loan(s). Similar to initial outlay but does not include the purchasing costs. Equity should increase over the life of the investment because of appreciation and loan amortization.

Equity dividend rate. See Cash-flow rate.

Evaluate. Analyze a property from an investment standpoint.

Face value. The amount of a loan as stipulated in the note. Face value is often different from the market value of the note due to below market interest rates.

Financial management rate of return (FMRR). A measure of investment performance applied to a property's projected cash flow.

Gross income. The potential or scheduled income from the property before payments for expenses or debt service.

Gross rent multiplier (GRM). The number that multiplied by the property's gross income results in an indication of market value for the property. Also, the name of this method of valuation.

Income statement. A statement that shows the income and expenses experienced or expected to be experienced by a property for a one-year period.

Indication of value. A final value estimate based on several preliminary indications of value.

Initial outlay. That amount of money (and any additional forms of consideration) put down to purchase the investment. Includes the cash down payment as well as closing costs incidental to the transaction. Exclusive of any loans or borrowed funds.

Investment analysis. The process of measuring an investment's expected performance.

Lender's yield. The return a lender expects to receive on a loan. In addition to including interest payment, yield can be enhanced by points, income participations, and so forth. Note that this term is applicable both to an institutional lender and to a seller who carries back a loan.

Leverage. Borrowed funds used in the purchase of a property to magnify the return on equity investment.

Liquidity. The measure of the ability to convert an investment into cash within a reasonably short period of time and at a reasonable price and terms.

Marginal tax rate. The tax rate of the bracket in which the investor's highest dollar of reportable income is found.

Market value. The top price a property will bring when sold under typical conditions and motivations.

Management. The act of conducting the business of a property to sustain an appropriate income. Strategies and intensity of management can vary according to the expertise and profit planning of the owner and manager.

Net operating income (NOI). Effective gross income less operating expenses. No deductions are made for loan payments or depreciation allowance. Also known as net income.

Net present value (NPV). An investment performance that measures the sum of the discounted cash flows in comparison to the initial outlay.

Net reversion. The amount the investor actually pockets from resale of the investment after deduction for sale costs, loan payoff, capital gains tax, and so forth.

Net sale price. Sale price less commissions, closing costs, title insurance, and other costs attributable specifically to the transaction itself. It does not include a deduction for loan payoffs or capital gains taxes.

Operating expenses. Those expenses required to keep the property open and producing a certain level of income. Includes such items as property taxes, utilities, repairs, and maintenance. It does not include loan payments or depreciation allowance.

Overall rate (OAR). A rate divided into the net operating income that results in an indication of value for a property. Mathematically, it is the percentage of sale price represented by net income. This figure can be abstracted from a comparable sale by dividing net income by sale price.

Point. A nonrefundable fee paid to the lender (usually by the borrower) to obtain a loan. Each point is 1% of the loan amount.

Present value (PV). The present lump-sum value of a future income or income stream such as cash flows from an investment. It will be less than merely the sum of the future cash flows since the future income is discounted to reflect time preference.

Rate of return. The annual rate of return or yield on the investor's initial outlay based on the resulting annual cash flows including the net reversion at resale. Two popular rates of return are the financial management rate of return and the internal rate of return.

Reconcile. To choose a final figure based on two or more indications of rent level, value, and so forth. This process requires judgment based on the reliability and applicability of the data involved and is usually concluded by rounding to the appropriate place. Not a mathematical averaging.

Reserves. An expense category used in a projected income statement to account for the replacement of short-lived items that are not accounted for elsewhere in the expenses.

Reversion. The sale price of a property (or total consideration received) upon resale.

Risk. The degree of uncertainty of possible income loss or other liability due to countless factors that can affect the investment.

Sale costs. Costs incidental to the sale of the property such as commissions, title insurance, legal fees, and so forth. The term does not include loan payoff or capital gain taxes.

Start. The beginning point or point of initial outlay in a series of annual projections.

Subject property. The property being valued or analyzed.

Tax payable. The amount of income taxes, if any, due the IRS (or any other taxing agency) by the investor as a result of taxable income generated by a particular investment.

Tax savings. The savings on income taxes, if any, that are a result of the tax shelter provided by a particular property.

Taxable income.   Income that is taxed. For real estate, taxable income is figured as annual gross income less operating expenses, interest payments, and depreciation.

Units of comparison.   Economic or physical units (income, units, rooms, etc.) that comparable sales are broken down into to make comparisons for the purpose of valuing a property.

Vacancy and collection loss (V&CL).   An allowance made when estimating income to compensate for vacancies and collection losses.

Valuate.   Determine the value of a property.

Value estimate.   An estimate of value for a property.

Value indicator.   See Units of comparison.

BIBLIOGRAPHY

Valuation

American Institute of Real Estate Appraisers, *Readings in the Income Approach to Real Property Valuation,* Vol. 1, Ballinger Publishing Company, Cambridge, MA, 1977.

American Institute of Real Estate Appraisers, *The Appraisal of Real Estate,* 7th ed., AIREA, Chicago, 1978.

Byrl N. Boyce, Ed., *Real Estate Appraisal Terminology,* American Institute of Real Estate Appraisers and the Society of Real Estate Appraisers, sponsors; Ballinger Publishing Company, Cambridge, MA, 1975.

Barbara Christensen, "Take the Guesstimating Out of Adjustments," *The Appraisal Journal,* April 1980, pp. 255–260.

Shannon L. Cutsinger, "Valuing Apartments with the Unit Mix Adjustment Technique," *The Real Estate Appraiser and Analyst,* May–June 1979, pp. 16–19.

Howard W. Dunham, "Real Estate Appraising From the Viewpoint of the Small Investor," *The Real Estate Appraiser and Analyst,* March–April 1979, pp. 31–36.

E. Roger Everett and William N. Kinnard, Jr., *A Guide To Appraising Apartments,* 5th ed., Society of Real Estate Appraisers, Chicago, 1979.

William C. Himstreet, *Writing Appraisal Reports,* American Institute of Real Estate Appraisers, Chicago, 1971.

William N. Kinnard, Jr., *Income Property Valuation,* Heath Lexington Books, Lexington, MA, 1971.

Kenneth M. Lusht, "Inflation and Real Estate Investment Value," *The Real Estate Appraiser and Analyst,* November–December 1979, pp. 11–16.

Society of Real Estate Appraisers, *A Guide to Narrative Demonstration Appraisal Reporting,* Chicago, 1976.

James R. Webb, "Negative Cash Flows: A Current Appraisal Problem," *The Appraisal Journal,* January 1981, pp. 95–101.

Investment Analysis

Charles B. Akerson, *The Internal Rate of Return in Real Estate Investments,* American Society of Real Estate Counselors, American Institute of Real Estate Appraisers, Chicago, 1976.

American Institute of Real Estate Appraisers, *Readings in Real Estate Investment Analysis,* Vol. 1, Ballinger Publishing Company, Cambridge, MA, 1977.

William R. Beaton and Terry Robertson, *Real Estate Investment,* 2nd ed., Prentice-Hall, Englewood Cliffs, NJ, 1977.

Wayne Etter, *"Leverage and the Real Estate Investor,"* Real Estate Review, Fall 1977, pp. 86–90.

M. Chapman Findlay, III and Stephen D. Messner, "Real Estate Investment Analysis: IRR Versus FMRR," *The Real Estate Appraiser,* July–August, 1975, pp. 5–20.

Gaylon E. Greer, *The Real Estate Investor and the Federal Income Tax,* John Wiley & Sons, New York, 1978.

Austin J. Jaffe and C. F. Sirmans, "Improving Real Estate Investment Analysis," *The Appraisal Journal,* January 1981, pp. 85–94.

William B. Martin, Jr., "A Risk Analysis Rate-of-Return Model for Evaluating Income-Producing Real Estate Investments," *The Appraisal Journal,* July 1978, pp. 424–442.

Maury Seldin and Richard H. Swesnick, *Real Estate Investment Strategy,* John Wiley & Sons, New York, 1978.

Douglas M. Temple, *Investing In Residential Income Property,* Contemporary Books, Chicago, 1974.

Gary M. Tenzer and Rocky A. Tarantello, "FMRR: A Programmable Calculator Implementation," *The Real Estate Appraiser and Analyst,* November–December 1979, pp. 11–16.

Donald J. Valachi, *"The Three Faces of IRR,"* Real Estate Review, Fall 1978, pp. 74–78.

Donald J. Valachi, "On Interpreting the Internal Rate of Return on a Real Estate Investment," *The Real Estate Appraiser and Analyst,* First Quarter 1981, pp. 35–42.

Finance

William Atteberry, *Modern Real Estate Finace,* 3rd ed., Grid Publishing, Inc., Columbus, OH, 1980.

G. Vincent Barrett, "Balancing the Benefits of the Tax-Deferred Exchange," *Real Estate Review,* Spring 1980, pp. 67–72.

William R. Beaton, *Real Estate Finance,* Prentice-Hall, Englewood Cliffs, NJ, 1975.

Edward T. Clare, *"All Inclusive Trust Deed: What's It Worth?"* California Real Estate, March 1980, pp. 28–30.

Wayne E. Etter, "Leverage and the Real Estate Investor," *Real Estate Review,* Fall 1977, pp. 86–90.

Jack P. Friedman and J. Bruce Lindeman, "Seller Financing and Cash Equivalence," *The Real Estate Appraiser and Analyst,* May–June 1979, pp. 46–50.

Gaylon E. Greer, *The Real Estate Investor and the Federal Income Tax,* John Wiley & Sons, New York, 1978.

Glenn V. Henderson, Jr. and William H. Walker, "Analysis of Installment Sales," *The Appraisal Journal,* October 1979, pp. 485–489.

J. Warren Higgins, "Installment Sales after the Installment Sales Revision Act of 1980," *The Real Estate Appraiser and Analyst,* First Quarter 1981, pp. 43–46.

Henry E. Hoagland and Leo D. Stone, *Real Estate Finance,* 5th ed., Richard D. Irwin, Inc., Homewood, IL, 1973.

Joseph B. Lipscomb, "Discount Rates for Cash Equivalent Analysis," *The Appraisal Journal,* January 1981, pp. 23–33.

Andrew James McLean, *Complete Guide to Real Estate Loans,* Delphi Information Sciences Corporation, 1980.

J. Thomas Montgomery, "Leverage," *The Appraisal Journal,* October 1977, pp. 589–600.

Daniel J. O'Connell, "What Is a Point Really Worth?" *Mortgage Banker,* March 1981, pp. 31–35. Reprinted in *Mortgage Banking Special Issue 1982,* pp. 48–51.

David Schoch, "Amortizing A Complex Wraparound," *Real Estate Review,* Winter 1981, pp. 17–18.

Allen F. Thomas, "Simplifying the Calculation of Yield on New Money," *Real Estate Review,* Spring 1979, pp. 81–84.

Donald J. Valachi, "The Tax-Deferred Exchange: Some Planning Considerations," *The Appraisal Journal,* January 1979, pp. 76–85.

INDEX